Since
Strangling
Isn't an Option...

⸺⧼∾∾∾⧽⸺

Dealing with Difficult
People—
Common Problems
and Uncommon Solutions

Sandra A. Crowe, M.A.

A PERIGEE BOOK

A PERIGEE BOOK
Published by the Penguin Group
Penguin Group (USA) Inc.
375 Hudson Street, New York, New York 10014, USA
Penguin Group (Canada), 90 Eglinton Avenue East, Suite 700, Toronto, Ontario M4P 2Y3, Canada (a division of Pearson Penguin Canada Inc.) • Penguin Books Ltd., 80 Strand, London WC2R 0RL, England • Penguin Group Ireland, 25 St. Stephen's Green, Dublin 2, Ireland (a division of Penguin Books Ltd.) • Penguin Group (Australia), 250 Camberwell Road, Camberwell, Victoria 3124, Australia (a division of Pearson Australia Group Pty. Ltd.) • Penguin Books India Pvt. Ltd., 11 Community Centre, Panchsheel Park, New Delhi—110 017, India • Penguin Group (NZ), 67 Apollo Drive, Rosedale, North Shore 0745, Auckland, New Zealand (a division of Pearson New Zealand Ltd.) • Penguin Books (South Africa) (Pty.) Ltd., 24 Sturdee Avenue, Rosebank, Johannesburg 2196, South Africa

Penguin Books Ltd., Registered Offices: 80 Strand, London WC2R 0RL, England

While the author has made every effort to provide accurate telephone numbers and Internet addresses at the time of publication, neither the publisher nor the author assumes any responsibility for errors, or for changes that occur after publication. Further, the publisher does not have any control over and does not assume any responsibility for author or third-party websites or their content.

First edition: October 1999

Library of Congress Cataloging-in-Publication Data

   Crowe, Sandra A.
      Since strangling isn't an option : dealing with difficult people—common problems and uncommon solutions / Sandra A. Crowe.—1st ed.
      p. cm.
      ISBN 978-0-399-52540-7
      1. Interpersonal conflict—I. Title.
      BF637.I48 .C76 1999
      158.2—dc21   99-41535
                                                               CIP

PRINTED IN THE UNITED STATES OF AMERICA

25   24   23   22   21   20   19   18

Most Perigee books are available at special quantity discounts for bulk purchases for sales promotions, premiums, fund-raising, or educational use. Special books, or book excerpts, can also be created to fit specific needs. For details, write: Special Markets, Penguin Group (USA) Inc., 375 Hudson Street, New York, New York 10014.

This book is dedicated
to those who live
from the highest.

Foreword

Recently, I was speaking with a client about her boss, whom she described as "worthy of strangling." When I asked what behavior had led her to that conclusion, she recounted an incident that said it all. She'd had a meeting with her boss at 2:00, and she arrived at 1:58 and 30 seconds. But when her boss looked at the clock and saw there was a minute and a half left to go, she said, "You're early. Come back at two." My client, feeling disregarded, dishonored, and downright disappointed, huffed subtly and went back to her desk to wait out the last minute in her office.

This kind of difficult, controlling behavior is a reflection of the times we live in. In the eight years since this book was originally published, much in our world has changed: the assault of September 11 on our country and the ensuing war in Iraq, the ever increasing rapidity of technology and the demands it puts on us, the threat of global warming, and the uphill business that seems to overtake our lives. This onslaught of external and internal stress leads people to look for ways to control situations and the people in them to the fullest extent possible.

One of the root creators of difficult behavior is stressors (financial, time, health, etc.). When the ability to cope with those stressors gets compromised, the individual reverts to the most available emotional response, which is usually negative, curt, or even offensive. When the behavior repeats itself, the recipe for difficult behavior has been set. We are in that game at the carnival where we keep getting dunked and we can't get back up fast enough. Our lives throw us back in again. Not only do we develop shorter fuses as a result of the inability to control the world and our lives, but everyone around us does as well.

But there are still aspects of life that are very much under our control. As we look to put the brakes on global warming for the planet, we can do the same with the internal warming and intensity of our relationships. Now more than ever we need strategies to help us deal. The principles in this book will help you cope in your personal and professional lives. If we see our relationships as reflections of ourselves, then dealing with others' personality differences is in effect healing us. But we cannot do this without awareness. If nothing else, that is what this book promises—the ability to name, pinpoint, and understand where difficult behavior comes from and what to do about it.

It is my heartfelt desire that this book will help you see your concerns with new eyes. I hope this reading journey leads you out of the "strangling" frustration of dealing with old perceptions, and into the freedom you long for. In the process, those difficulties will shift, not because others did, but because you did.

Blessings for creating the healthy relationships you deserve.

Sandra A. Crowe
Bethesda, MD, 2007

Contents

viii   *Contents*

Preface

It's 1983. I've just graduated from UNC–Chapel Hill (Yes, Michael Jordan was also there but he doesn't talk about it) and I'm headed for Africa, where I will spend the better part of a year. In Africa, my boycott of malaria vaccines finally catches up with me, and I come close to meeting my maker. So I head home to Charlottesville, Virginia, to recuperate. When I'm back on my feet, I set out for Washington, D.C., in search of a job that will pay my way back to Africa. I waitress, serve a stint as a court reporter, and learn the catering business. Finally, I give up on Africa and decide to take on the world of advertising.

Armed with a cardboard dummy and an idea, I trudge round and round Dupont Circle, cajoling and coaxing store owners to buy space on my cardboard. I promise to transfer their ads onto state-of-the-art place mats—the answer to all their advertising problems. It works. My first place mat sells out in days. I hawk my place mat idea for a year and a half. Now I'm bored.

With a pair of comfortable shoes and 10,000 brochures,

I march down to the corner of Connecticut Avenue in the middle of downtown D.C. to test my next business venture. At the top of my lungs I yell, "POWERLUNCH! GET YOUR POWERLUNCH!" The idea is this: You tell me the type of businessperson you want to meet, and I arrange for you to have lunch with him. You pay for lunch, plus a fee for the setup. Now I'm a business matchmaker. I spend my last pennies getting this together—it better work!

After the third day of yelling, I drag myself home. No one's called. Now I'm broke *and* devastated. As I walk in the door, the phone rings. A *Washington Post* reporter has seen the brochure and wants an interview. The next day, I have lunch with him. At the end of our conversation, he asks for my business phone number. "Hmm," I say. "Let me get back to you on that." I leave him, race to the phone company, and secure the number, the last four digits of which spell out EATT. When I call him back with the number, he likes it so much he puts it in the story.

Two days later a friend calls at 8 A.M.: "Congratulations! You're on the front page of the *Washington Post* 'Style' section."

"Oh no," I think. "My phone isn't hooked up yet." Then there's a knock on the door. It's the telephone installer. She goes up on the pole, and a few minutes later comes back down and gives me a piece of paper.

"What's this?" I ask. "They're the messages I took while I was on the pole hooking up your number," she explains. My business takes off. The press coverage brings calls from people all around the country. In the beginning, I match people one-on-one, then in groups. I launch POW-ERLUNCH! Network nights where hundreds of people meet. (The success of POWERLUNCH! is recounted in the book *Chicken Soup for the Soul at Work*.)

This goes on for two years. Then one night a man asks me to market him and his seminars. I accept, and soon my life's purpose begins to unfold. He teaches me how to help people become more aware of their behavior, thought, and action. I go back to school, get a master's degree in applied psychology, and I've been leading seminars ever since. My clients have included the White House Personnel Office, Sony Corporation, Citicorp, Marriott, The Discovery Channel, NASA, Intelsat, COMSAT, the Departments of the Army and Navy, the Social Security Administration, and many associations and colleges.

In 1995, I completed an ontological coaching program. The influence of my mentors, Julio and Rafael, is evident throughout this book. So I give you the product of the past ten years of my personal and professional experience. I hope it gives you greater awareness, shows you that life is full of choices, and points you down the path of strength and peace. Happy reading.

Note: If you would like to contact me directly with feedback on the book or for more information about what I do, e-mail me at sc@pivpoint.com or check out my website at www.pivpoint.com.

Introduction: Eyesight to the Blind

Did you ever feel like the only fire hydrant in a town full of dogs? When people in our lives are being difficult, we tend to see ourselves as a fire hydrant. It's so easy to complain about what's being done to us. We just stand there fastened to the curb and people relieve themselves on us. But once we recognize that how we react affects how they are with us, we can unscrew the bolts that keep us immobilized, victimized, and rooted in unproductive relationships. Relationships are difficult, but they are also inherently wonderful. I promise to help you find the wonderful within the difficult, to bring perspective and solution to chaos and conflict and to help you see the light in your dark encounters with difficult people. If you'd never been awake during daylight, you might not be able to imagine the sun. Not because it doesn't exist, but because you hadn't seen it. Are you ready for the sun?

This book will help you examine the challenging people in your sphere, understand why they act the way they do, evaluate how you react to them, and learn how to deal with difficult situations when you can't find ways to pre-empt them. In the process it will help you discover more about yourself. The relationship you have with yourself will change, your self-awareness will increase, and you will become more authentic in your relationship with yourself as well as others.

What does it mean when your relationships change? What expectations do you have? If you solve your problems with difficult people at work, do you think you'll be promoted to vice-president? Drive a fabulous car? Suddenly become happy in your marriage?

Are your expectations realistic? Will having an easier time with your difficult people make you happier?

What will be the outcome? What's the benefit of getting along with others, especially those who make us miserable? What will resolving relationship issues give you? Will you get a thing called happiness? Will you sleep better at night? What do you expect to gain? The more you know about what you want, the more this book can help you.

New Habits

Interlace your fingers. Which thumb is on top? Now pull them apart and interlace them again. Same thumb on top? For most people it will be, because it's their habit.

Habits can be healthy or harmful, but they get us into trouble when it comes to difficult people. Typically our habits with difficult people are negative. Habits and repetitive patterns of thought and action increase our frustration. How do we replace our bad habits with good ones?

Most difficult people's actions and reactions are born from subconscious habitual patterns. Difficult people are generally unaware of how they affect others. Take Sam as an example. For three months, Jack worked for Sam on a display booth for a street fair. Sam thought that as a boss it was perfectly acceptable to yell at people. He'd been like this for years and had always gotten away with it because people put up with it.

When Sam wielded his authority, Jack would act passively, biting back his anger, or aggressively, yelling till he grew hoarse. One night Sam got so angry he told Jack to go home. "I'll do the job myself," he bellowed. Jack wanted to scream back, but this time he realized the situation had gone too far. Jack decided to be assertive, instead of passive or aggressive as usual.

"This is not okay. You can't talk to me like this," Jack told him calmly but sternly. "No one deserves to be treated the way you treat people. You need to be right all the time. Stuff happens and you overreact."

Sam was stunned. At first his face tightened, his lips curled, and he prepared to counterattack. But then he stopped and calmed down. He wasn't expecting Jack's new behavior. He froze, unable to react. He thought about what Sam had said. From that moment on, he couldn't look at himself the same way.

What changed this scenario was Jack's reaction to Sam: how he handled *himself* more than how he handled Sam. For the first time he stood up for himself, he expressed his frustration, and demanded to be treated with dignity. When Jack realized his new response led to the desired outcome, he decided to try this new pattern in other relationships. Before he knew it, it became his new habit.

The last days they spent together passed smoothly. They worked together better than ever before. At the end of the project, Sam wished Jack luck and they went their separate ways. Jack left with a new habit. And so did Sam.

How do we move out of our negative habits? Recognize and acknowledge we don't know what we don't know. In her book *Everyday Zen*, Charlotte Joko Beck says, "What we want to do is to find some way of working with the basic insanity that exists because of our blindness." When we're distraught and wrung out over our difficult relationships, we can't see other ways of dealing with them. Our anger and frustration cloud our vision, and we're blinded by them. Often we can't see the way we operate because we're so caught up in the emotions. This blindness creates insanity. And insanity is commonly known as doing the same thing over and over again and expecting a different result.When we repeatedly encounter difficult people and don't change our behavior, we are, in a way, blind and insane. We're like rats on a treadmill.

Applying the principles of this book will help us get off

the belt, and stop running in place. How do we shed new light on old problems? How do we wipe away the obstacles to clear vision? How do we stop feeling sorry for ourselves and realize that we have choices in life? The answers are critical to restructuring our relationships and finding peace.

Albert Einstein said, "We cannot solve a problem at the level at which it was created." We need to go to new levels to solve these problems. Dig deeper to uncover what is hidden; rise higher to gain a different perspective.

What makes this book different from any other is the two-prong perspective: "What am I doing?," which is internal, and "What are they doing?," which is external. Stephen Covey in *The 7 Habits of Highly Effective People* says, "Change—real change—comes from the inside out. It doesn't come from hacking at the leaves of attitude and behavior with quick fix personality ethic techniques. It comes from striking at the root—the fabric of our thought, the fundamental, essential paradigm, which gives definition to our character and creates the lens through which we see the world." It's like the Zen master who steps up to the hot dog stand and says, "Make me one with everything."

The hot dog vendor then fixes a hot dog and hands it to the Zen master, who pays with a $20 bill. The hot dog vendor puts the bill in the cash drawer and closes the drawer.

"Where's my change?" asks the Zen master.

The hot dog vendor responds, "Change must come from within."

*   *   *

Use this book as a guide for developing the skill to change your inner and outer abilities to deal with difficult people in business, in society, or at home.

We will also operate from the two-sided approach of understanding and action. By understanding why other people act the way they do and how you respond, you can stop the negative cycle. Are you ready to stop difficult people from ruining your day? Are you willing to give up old ways of thinking in order to have new freedom in your relationships? Do you want a permanent solution to your people problems? The time is right. Your destiny is waiting . . .

PART ONE

Fundamentals of Understanding

Learning is finding out that you already know. Doing is demonstrating that you know it. Teaching is reminding others that they know just as well as you. You are all learners, doers, and teachers.

—Richard Bach

ONE

The Disease of Difficultness: It's All in Your Head

There is no such thing as a problem without a gift for you in its hands. You seek problems because you need their gifts.

—*Richard Bach, author of* Illusions

The Seeds Are Planted

Do you cross the road, not to get to the other side, but to avoid a difficult person? Have your personal or professional goals been interrupted by someone's incompetence? Are you spending too much physical and emotional energy wading through the conflicts? Need relief and you've run out of Alka-Seltzer? If the answer to any of these questions is yes, you've come to the right place. Help is here.

Think of yourself as a gardener trying to cultivate healthy, productive relationships. You're clawing at the hard earth with your fingers, your furrows are uneven, and the soil is not tilled deeply enough. You need a tool, something strong, sturdy, and reliable, that you can turn to time and again to get the job done. This book is your all-purpose hoe.

By reading this book, you've already taken two major steps toward coping with difficult people: You've recognized that you need to deal with this issue, and you've acquired a resource to help you improve your relationships. This isn't rocket science; it's a matter of looking at the conflicts in your life from a different perspective. The value is in *re-minding*; it's a matter of tapping your own strength, focusing on it, and redirecting it. Are you ready for this part of your life to be different? Can you look honestly at yourself and take stock of your own behavior? If your answer is yes, here are a few questions to consider as you enter into this commitment with yourself: How much does the difficult relationship mean to you? Can solving the problem be as simple as switching bank accounts to avoid a testy teller? Or does your career depend upon smoothing out contacts with a difficult person? Are you open to new approaches to your difficult relationships? Can you change in order to make them work? Are you willing to put your ego on hold in order to make it happen?

Difficult people cause us great trouble when our actions are tied to, or linked with, theirs. Sometimes when people work together in an office, the parties involved are likely to feel as though their co-workers are more like opponents than team members. When this happens, we chafe at the very thought of having our product, and our reputation, influenced by someone the company has thrust upon us.

As personal-development guru Tony Robbins says, "The questions you ask yourself determine your destiny." Have you asked yourself: "Why am I having this experience? What can I do to learn from it? What opportunity is this person presenting to me?" Can you see this person as a teacher and the experience as a chance to gain new insights about yourself?

Pretend you're leaving your job. When you prepare your résumé for your next position you will list all your skills and achievements. The way you overcame your problems with your difficult person can certainly be counted as an asset. What can you learn from this conflict? This person is presenting you with the chance to improve yourself. By looking at this situation as a learning opportunity, you will undoubtedly change the way you behave and react.

Once you've determined that the value of this experience is an opportunity to learn, the second question is: "What does this say about me? What is this person reflecting to me about me that I haven't yet learned?" In other words, "Why does this bother me so much and what can I do about it?"

Before you decide what you're going to do to fix things, you must really look inside and take responsibility for the situation, for your role in it, and for your reaction to it. By the end of this book you will see that the key to success with difficult people is in changing your response to them. One of the best ways to begin doing that is to assess your attitude in dealing with them.

How's Your Attitude?

We all assess our own overall attitudes as positive and productive, but few people are confident and upbeat all the time. Before diagnosing a problem, a doctor will often do a baseline blood test. Having a baseline will determine whether or not remedies work when the doctor compares it to future results. Let's do a quiz to assess your present or baseline attitude. After you've read the book, come back and take it again to see how your results have changed.

Baseline Attitude Level

YES or NO?

_____   *I interact daily with negative people and feel drained.*

_____   *I am influenced by negative people.*

_____   *I read the newspaper.*

_____   *I get angry at least once a day.*

_____   *Things at home could be better.*

_____   *I wake up irritated.*

_____   *There's not much to look forward to.*

_____   *There are people out to get me.*

_____   *The little things that go wrong irritate me.*

_____   *I live for Friday.*

_____   *I watch more than two hours of TV each day.*

_____   *I never overlook flaws in people or situations.*

If you had two or fewer yes answers, your attitude is good. You have fun, surround yourself with positive people, and enjoy life.

If you answered yes to between three and six statements, don't despair; there is hope.

More than seven yes answers indicates you may need help. You need some guidance in finding a different path to follow. Applying the principles in this book will help you change this attitude and ultimately your reaction to others around you. These changes will help turn your misery into joy.

You are what you think, and you become what you focus on. Do you focus on negative or positive things? Do you appreciate life or complain about it? Do you know that changing your focus changes your world?

Worry Warts

Part of the reason we have such problems with people is that worry actually makes the situation worse than it is. Worry is about the future, about what might be, and mostly about what isn't. Are you sweating under a cloak of worry? Have you noticed how worrying influences your ability to act rationally with someone? Unchecked worry grows into panic, so it is better to acknowledge it than to let it run rampant. Typical worrisome thoughts might be: "I'm never going to get this right," "This will only get worse," or "I'm doomed." Focusing on the cause of the worry only gets us more of what we already have, so thinking about that difficult person or situation is like a growing virus. How can we begin to move out of the mind-set of worry, which is often so much worse than the situation itself?

The secret to moving out of the sinkhole of worry is to change not so much what you are thinking, but the way you are thinking. Charlotte Joko Beck, author of *Everyday Zen*, says that we give too much importance to the connection between our own self-concept and the thoughts we have. In other words, we make statements like "I'm worried about the meeting tomorrow," instead of "This thought is: worry about meeting tomorrow." Reframing our approach from "I am thinking . . ." to "The thought is . . ." may seem like hair-splitting, but it raises an important point, one of temporary vs. permanent thinking. If we see our thoughts as temporary it empowers us to allow our thinking to change and to react differently. Operating from the "I" perspective reinforces our separateness. It literally divides the world into "you" versus "everyone else" when in fact, we are more alike than we are different.

Once you have the thought, or the assessment, of "I think you are like this," you have married the concept of "I" and the concept of your thought together. Now there is an attachment and an interest in maintaining the validity of your opinion. By putting a little space between you and the thoughts you have, you step away from personalizing things. If you can detach yourself from the thought, and realize it is only a thought, you buy yourself the freedom to change that thought. As the new thoughts pile up you can reevaluate—and begin to change—the way you think and assess situations. After all, nobody can see things exactly as they are. We are all dependent on our perceptions.

Then when you notice that you are worrying, think: "This is worrying." When you do this, fully notice and experience the feelings, bodily reactions (such as nail biting and nervous tics), and recurrent thoughts. Write down repetitive thoughts as if you're dumping them on a piece of paper and off your mind. This shift will allow you to think about the process of worry, rather than what you're afraid of. The tension will release as you step back from it, and then you can think more rationally. As Swami Anantananda says in his book *What's on My Mind*, "Do not ask circumstance to give you equipoise; give equipoise to circumstance." In other words, after you fully experience and acknowledge your present state, your next step should be to move to a new, more productive one.

Your worst fears may yet materialize, but worrying about them is detrimental to your life now. Some people are afraid that the world is going to end. What happens if they get to the end of the world and realize they wasted the little time they had left worrying about it? The truth is, worry rarely changes anything. It allows a future event, or the possibility of that event, to infect the present. By beginning to examine how our mind works, we can see how the negative cycles of the mind pull us down. These negative cycles prevent us from knowing what is truly before us. What can we know? How can we use that knowledge to redirect the future?

A Change of Focus

WHEN LINDA WENT into the hospital to give birth to her first child, American troops were girding for conflict in the Middle East. The faraway battle and the threat of terrorism at home filled her with panic, but so did the idea of becoming a mother.

During the five days Linda spent in the hospital recovering from a cesarean section, she was glued to the TV, unable to turn away even when friends visited. She watched through the small hours of the night when she should have been sleeping. For those few days, her whole world narrowed to an eight-by-ten-foot room and the missile strikes of the Iraq War.

Linda was so focused on the coverage of the war, and the media's sensational response to it, that she was surprised when she drove home. People were jogging, working, riding the subway, and going about their normal business. As far as she could tell from her hospital window, life had stopped, and she thought that everyone else was huddled around their TV sets, just like her.

Because she had focused on this one dark spot, it grew and grew until it blotted out everything else, blotted out the light, and threw her into a cold shadow. The world had become as she had seen it. It wasn't until she got home and turned her attention to the new baby that the anxiety she felt about the war dissipated. She changed her focus, and in turn changed her world.

Knowing What We Know

We think we know how life is, but we only know how we observe it, and everything is altered when it runs through our filters. We think that what we see or believe to be true is perceived the same way by everyone. Often we fail to factor in our perspective. People's perceptions of others or situations can be influenced by their upbringing, values, religion, race, and so on. To understand others we must understand ourselves better, and see the line where the tangible truth blends into our interpretation of the truth. Then we can begin to see how we judge others.

What we experience and how we speak about our experiences is colored by many factors. For instance, I couldn't be a brain surgeon because I don't have the particular knowledge that a brain surgeon does. If I were to cut open someone's skull, I would see a mass of blood and goo. A brain surgeon would see the intricate interplay of tissue and veins that compose the powerful and mysterious control center of the human animal. He or she would also detect damage or malformations that the untrained eye would never recognize.

The observer that the surgeon has become through his or her training is quite different from the observer that I am. It is important to ask yourself, "What kind of an observer am I?" Often, what we see is what we have sought. This is a difficult concept to understand and apply because we are blinded by our past experiences and by what we accept as reality. The old Yiddish expression "On an elephant you can see a flea but on yourself you can't see an elephant" comes to mind as we acknowledge how important, yet challenging, this concept is. By exploring solutions to problems with difficult people, we expand our opportunity to be a different observer.

Playing Favorites

You and Sally share an office, and you both deal with John. John is a difficult person to you, but he is a wonderful person to Sally. Is John really a difficult person? For you the answer is yes, because you perceive him as difficult. For Sally the answer is no.

What happens if you change the observer you are? Will John still appear difficult?

It's possible that John is reacting differently to you than to Sally. If you examine how you observe the situation, and find that this is indeed the case, then you need to explore why he acts differently with you. Because Sally isn't having any problems with him, the difficulty is likely to be inherent in your relationship. What are you doing or not doing that could be causing him to act this way? Are there any factors in your interactions with him that are just simply not an issue in his relationship with Sally?

Look at Sally. What is she doing that works? Can you model her behavior? Act as if you like John. Make believe your problems with him never happened. Clean the slate, and start over. What new behavior will you elicit? Imagine

Chocolate Obsession

I TOLD A FRIEND that I didn't care for a particular piece of chocolate I'd eaten. He couldn't believe that I could tell the difference between one brand of chocolate and another. He thought that chocolate is chocolate, and that there is no difference in taste from one brand to another. He was so convinced that I couldn't tell chocolates apart that he challenged me to a contest.

With guests at a party as witnesses, he blindfolded me and offered me four samples he'd bought from Israel, England, Switzerland, and the United States. If I could tell them apart and identify them, he would treat me to dinner at the restaurant of my choice. If I failed, dinner would be on me.

As I slowly took each piece I allowed its smell, texture, and essence to enter my nose and mouth. I closed my eyes and focused on the experience of the morsel. I moved each bit from side to side and let it roll over my tongue. Swiss milk chocolate has an unparalleled smoothness to it, and I was able to identify it by its texture. American chocolate has a brash sweetness that makes the top of my nose tingle, and it is usually crafted in thin bars. English chocolate has a sour sweetness to it that always leaves me just a bit unsatisfied, and Israeli chocolate was the only one left.

As you might have guessed, he took me to dinner—at an expensive French restaurant. He lost the bet. However, he gained some insight—the knowledge that others are able to perceive the world quite differently from the way he perceives it.

yourself taking your bad feelings and putting them in a box. (You can always take them out again if you have to.) By modeling the behaviors that work for others, we see life from their perspective. It's often hard to imagine that others see the world so differently, but when we realize this, our judgments fall away, we relax, and life gets easier. Your view of the world is your view, no more, no less. It isn't your burden to convince others that you're absolutely right or know "the truth."

Awareness Alert

When you become uneasy in any situation I suggest you do these three things: (1) Become aware of your emotional state; (2) let others know how you feel; and (3) propose other options to move through or out of the situation. What is your state? Close your eyes and touch what's going on within. Ask yourself, What's your emotional barometer? Am I: Anxious? Tired? Bored? Frustrated? How am I breathing? How was my day? Am I still "wearing" it? If someone were to say something irritating to me right now, how would I react? Cry? Not care? Get upset? The purpose of this exercise is to help you recognize your sore spots before someone else touches them. Ask yourself these questions as you begin your day and then take note of how the answers change. What changes them? Is it events (external) or your thoughts about them (internal)?

Once you're aware of your emotional state you can let others know when your threshold is low. Simply saying

"I'm having a tough day" will inspire people to have compassion for you and to restrict the emotional issues they expect you to deal with. You may even solicit help. At the very least, others will know they aren't the source of your problems.

Alerting people when your threshold is low is one way to offset potential explosions. Another is to be compassionate with others, whose thresholds may be low. You can offer them options: "Should I call you back about this next week?" "Would you like me to let this issue go?" "Maybe I can work out some of the bugs and get back to you further along in the process." These are ways to let them know you're aware of their feelings.

Now that you've got a keener idea of how you operate from the neck up, what are some things you can do to get the rest of you moving out of difficult situations? It's time to take the lid off your trash can of difficult stories. The best way to do that is to grab the handle . . .

TWO

Get Me Outta Here:
Escape Hatches

A Physics Lesson

Human relationships, however brief or superficial, follow Newton's third law: For every action there is an equal and opposite reaction. The key is to recognize the action (the difficult person's behavior) and the reaction (your patterned response to it).

We are creatures of habit. We develop these ingrained responses to other people's words or actions to the point where we lose touch with why they happen. All we know is that we become angry or irritated. One woman in a recent seminar said that just the thought of her difficult person was enough to get her blood boiling. Can you imagine what happened when that person actually walked into the room?

The Law of Outcome

Event (no control) + Response (control) = Outcome

When an event occurs that is beyond your control, the response you have is still within your control, as difficult as that may be to believe you are responsible for your reactions. It is important to think of the two parts of the equation as separate. The event is independent of your response. Different people will respond to the same situation differently. Take the case of two people riding a roller coaster: One feels a rush of excitement, while the other may become nauseated.

Since you can't control the events, you must look at how you're responding, why you're responding that way, and how you can respond more productively for a better outcome.

The key to changing, and to behaving more productively, is understanding. First, notice what your difficult person is doing, and when he or she is doing it. Second, notice how, when, and why you're reacting with automatic responses such as yelling, cursing, insulting, and other bloodcurdling, childish immediate reactions. Replay the exchange in your mind and note it in a journal. As you examine the exchange, you will first notice yourself remembering to change your behavior *after* the interaction. Then you will begin to remember to change your behavior *while* you are interacting with that person. Finally, you will catch yourself changing your behavior *before* interacting with him or her.

As you continue to gain awareness and understanding of your difficult person and your response to him or her, doors will begin to open, and through them lights will shine that will guide you on your path to a solution. If you turn the keys to these doors and open them wide, you will change your thinking and change the way you deal with difficult people. Your ability to control your feelings will grow and, in turn, the difficulties will diminish.

Have you committed to doing whatever it takes to resolve your issues with difficult people? Have you decided that you can let go of your pride, your ego, and your need to be right for the sake of peace and resolution? If so, passing through these doors will help you achieve that goal.

Ten Doors and One Window

Door #1: Change Yourself and Your World Changes

What do you need to do differently to have the people around you appear different? Remember, perception is reality.

When I was a kid, my mother used to yell across the house: "Sandy, where are you? What are you doing?"

That question drove me crazy. I would invariably respond, "I'm here. Leave me alone." She would then yell a few more things my way and I would yell a few more things back.

Recently my mother and her boyfriend came to my house for a visit. It had been a while since I'd seen them, so they decided to stay for the day. They settled in to watch TV, and I went to my office to sort through some mail.

Moments after I left the room I heard my mother scream, "Sandy, where are you? What are you doing?" I left my body. Or I at least shrank in it. In that moment I became a seven-year-old girl, indignant and furious at her mother for asking meddlesome questions and invading her privacy.

Just as I was about to respond (in that seven-year-old way), my awareness kicked in. I noticed what I was about to do and stopped. I realized that I am an adult now, not a child, and remembered that I have choices. I took a breath, cleared my throat, and said, "I'm up here, Mom, going through the mail." She then said, "Oh, okay." End of exchange, altercation averted.

My mother looked different to me in that moment. She looked nicer, gentler, less suffocating than she ever had before. I was not oppressed, so she was not oppressive. I felt more appreciation and love for her than I had in a long time. I remember thinking to myself, "Boy she sure has changed." But what really happened was that I had changed. I had consciously changed my response to a question that had previously infuriated me. It's as easy as changing your thinking.

Door #2: Negative Out, Negative In

Have you noticed how you feel after having been around complainers and negative people? Negative people influence us more than we realize. As much as you can control it, stop being negative yourself (stop thinking negative thoughts) and change the company you hang around with.

You're stuck with your boss, you say? He may be out there, but he is not inside you. Don't let him in. Imagine that you're a brick wall, and your boss is coming at you like an angry bull, nostrils flaring and eyes ablaze. What happens when his momentum meets your righteousness? Crash! But what if you were an iron gate instead of a brick wall? Could you allow room for him to act out his agression on you without allowing it to have any impact on you, literally or figuratively?

If you do find yourself around negative people and you can't (or aren't prepared to) break away, then offset negativity with positiveness. Allow your pure light to deflect the darkness that negative people intend to infect you with. Wear your good attitude like armor. Find inspirational writing to read at bedtime (for suggested reading check the Bibliography); listen to positive words on the way to work; and surround yourself with nurturing people as much as possible. This will at least neutralize the difficult person's toxic effect on you. Get out of as many negative situations as you can—your mental and physical health is worth it.

Next, ask yourself what your options really are. Perhaps you think that removing yourself from the situation would mean admitting defeat, and you've avoided requesting a transfer or trying to work on other projects. Maybe you are just plain scared of the prospect of leaving a job. Maybe you would rather endure the drawbacks of one situation than gamble on the unknowns of another.

One of my first real jobs was with a company that treated me horribly. My employers paid me a paltry salary, sent me on trips with less than a day's notice, were rude to me, and ignored my requests. I didn't think I could get a job anywhere else, so I took the abuse until one day I couldn't take it anymore. I quit.

It was one of the happiest days of my life. Although I was petrified of what would happen next, I was relieved of the burden of the office. If I hadn't jumped, I might never have been available for the rewarding, uplifting, and energizing experiences that followed. And I recognized that the whole course of events was a great lesson.

Door #3: Reward and Discourage

Have you ever seen rats in a maze? They quickly learn the route through the maze when they find a treat at the end, and wander aimlessly through the labyrinth if there is no reward.

If you don't like what someone is saying or doing, don't laugh, smile, or behave in any way that can be construed as approval. Remember that some people think of raising your ire as a reward. Instead, ignore the comment or calmly voice your objections. Like the rats, once difficult people find your button, they like to push it regularly.

In one of my seminars, a woman who had been part of a team for ten years said that a team member had often made inappropriate jokes that she found particularly offensive. I asked how people responded to this verbal abuse, and she explained that they laughed uncomfortably even though they all disliked this person's idea of humor. But nobody could figure out why he continued to behave so rudely.

When we talked about the reward of laughter, she saw how they had all unwittingly encouraged this person. She asked the other members to ignore the remarks, and when they did the rude comments diminished and eventually stopped.

The lesson is this: Reward the behavior you'd like to see repeated, and discourage the behavior you want to stop.

Hidden Rewards

The difficult person is receiving a reward for his behavior. If he wasn't, he wouldn't be doing it. You may not see the benefits, and they may not seem like rewards to you. Unfortunately, it is not always easy to identify the benefit or reward because they can take on different forms, from the obvious to the most construed, even negative consequences.

So you may ask yourself: Is it about control? About manipulation? Putting you down? Laughing at your expense? Humiliating you? Attracting or deflecting attention? Blaming you for his shortcomings? Avoiding you? Overcoming your objections or dismissing your ideas? Taking credit for your ideas? Catching you off guard? Acting on his feelings but not discussing them?

Ask yourself what this person gains by being difficult with you. Once you've identified the reward, you can work on removing it.

Door #4: The Stronger of Two Emotions Will Dominate

Have you ever encountered someone who was in a nasty mood when you were in a neutral one? When two people meet, the person who feels his or her particular state of mind more passionately will pour those feelings out to the other.

The other day I walked into the doctor's office in a bad mood. I swung the door open and approached the receptionist. "I'm so happy you're here!" she said. I politely thanked her, but I still felt grumpy.

She smiled warmly and told me it had been too long since she'd seen me. As her enthusiasm and sunniness beamed from her, the warmth she radiated penetrated my gloom like the sun poking through the clouds. Soon the clouds cleared altogether. My low mood was pulled up to her high one. I started feeling lighter, and returned her smile with a genuine one of my own.

Michael Deaver, former White House Deputy Chief of Staff under President Reagan, had the honor of meeting Mother Teresa. When he asked why she had given so much of herself to the world, she whispered, "The greatest gift in the world is giving." She told him a story about a grungy, dirty, starved man of the street who was brought to her by the nuns. He was so weak that he could barely lift his head to see her looking at him. Mother Teresa washed him, removing the dirt and neglect of the world from his head. Mike asked her, "Why, why do you do this?" She looked intently into his eyes and asked, "Have you ever seen half a smile?"

Half a smile doesn't exist; it's like being half pregnant. Mother Teresa's reward was someone else's happiness. She herself exuded love and happiness. She exemplified it, created it by her actions, and fed it to others who had the good fortune to be in her presence. Because the stronger of two emotions dominates, just being in her sphere had the power to change one's thinking. We all have that power with one another.

What is your emotion right now? The next time you encounter your difficult person, notice the moment at which your emotion shifts. Does the mere thought of her send you reeling into the emotional abyss? Does it happen when you see her? After words have passed between you? What does she say or do that changes your state? If you can identify triggers, those irritating behaviors that send you into overdrive, your ability to shift back will become greater.

Your awareness is like a muscle. Develop it the same way you would any other muscle in your body. Use it over and over again. Focus on it. Put all of your attention on it. Become aware of your awareness and exercise it.

This is what will lead you to freedom from your difficult people.

Door #5: The One Who Understands Guides or Controls

If you understand the other person better than he understands himself, you can control the communication.

Suppose that no matter what you wear, your difficult person finds fault. Sometimes she gives you questionable compliments: "Nice dress. Too bad it's magenta." "That would look great on someone thinner." "I saw that in a magazine two years ago."

You react by blowing up. You hurl insults back. Before long, your exchange moves beyond your garments and into your personal grooming, your choice of friends, or your IQ. And this is how your relationship is, time after time.

The next time she approaches you with her wardrobe review, stop for a moment. Say to yourself, "Look what she's doing. She's going to say something insulting to make me react."

The person who understands what is occurring guides or controls the situation, and once you understand that her goal is to get your goat, then you are in a position of control, instead of simply reacting.

Based on what you understand, and your memory of previous encounters with this person, you can choose not to respond in your usual way, and blow her expectations out of the water. Then the interaction begins and ends with her condemnation, and you can go on to do something different.

Know yourself. At what moment does the button get pushed? Can you see it coming? If you can, you will avoid being manipulated and bulldozed.

Sometimes the things people say to us irritate us because we hear words without appreciating the intention behind them. Recently I mentioned to a friend that I wasn't feeling well. He offered his sympathy and compassion by saying: "Poor baby." What he had meant as tenderness, I took as a condescending insult. I said, "Don't say 'poor baby' to me!" I would have preferred if he had offered some hope, saying something like "You'll be better soon," rather than encouraging my sorry state.

What he didn't know—what he couldn't have known—was that his response reminded me of how my family had pitied me when I was sick. I was trying to move beyond that to a more enlightened attitude. I was already wallowing in self-pity, and his words made it worse.

Soon I realized the source of my anger, and I asked him to repeat the phrase so that I could desensitize myself to it, and to strip it of its power over me. He looked at me with uncertainty, and then he began to repeat "Poor baby" over and over until I became immune. Those words have little effect on me today.

Door #6: Don't Order People to Change—
Invite Them to Change

What people resist about change is being changed. They want to be enticed and supported, but not forced. They like to think that changes in their behavior are born of their own motivation to be better people, and they want to take credit for their own growth. They don't want to be made to change; they want to make the change themselves and they want to think it was their idea.

We find it easy to tell people what we don't like about them or how they should be different. But it would be more effective to emphasize a strength and illustrate how a person's action will result in a benefit. For example, instead of saying, "You lazy slob. Can't you make a single meeting on time?," try, "Your input is so valuable. I think its really important that you get to the meeting on time so you can share your ideas." And instead of firing back hurtful insults you might try saying, "Your comments really hurt my feelings. I think we would be more productive if we could create an atmosphere of respect."

This won't always work. Eighty percent of the population responds to rewards. The other 20 percent may require a more direct approach. Sometimes it's necessary to say, "Be here on time for the next meeting," because certain people are used to being addressed that way and won't respond otherwise. What motivates them may not make sense to you, so you may have to go against your

CLOSE TO HOME   JOHN McPHERSON

E:CLOSETOHOME@COMPUSERVE.COM   4-3

© 1997 John McPherson
/Dist. by Universal Press Syndicate

www.uexpress.com

"He learned how to climb out, so
we greased the crib."

own instincts when dealing with these types. Remember, if what you're doing isn't working, try something else.

The Ripple Effect of Change

Has anyone ever asked you to change the way you did things, then didn't like it when you complied? While your inability to please this person may be disappointing and frustrating for you, it also indicates the other person is faced with having to change him/herself in response to you.

Looking at the other side of the coin, you may find that when someone changes at your request, you still have to make changes in yourself. Be careful what you ask for, and be careful how you respond when you get it. For instance, a friend complained that her husband wasn't sensitive to her needs. She complained to him and he began to change, but she continued to be dissatisfied. She didn't know how to react to his new behavior. She had to change something about herself. Her old ways didn't work with his new ways. She continued to complain, even though he had changed to accommodate her.

Door #7: Go to Oz and Get a Heart

Have compassion. Even the people you consider cooperative do things for their own reasons, and not yours. Whatever experiences people have create filters, and those filters color the way they look at the world. Don't judge until you have walked in another man's moccasins, . . . his booties, his saddle shoes, his sneakers, his flip-flops or his loafers. Give them the benefit of the doubt. In many cases the scuffs and gouges in those old shoes determine whether he will shuffle around in the shadows or strut like a preening peacock. His experiences of yesterday determines his behavior of today.

What experiences brought your difficult person to his or her unstable emotional place? Asking yourself that question and wondering about the answer will make you more compassionate. Remember that grocery store clerk who rolled her eyes and clucked her tongue because your canned ham didn't have a price on it? What was your reaction? Did you think she was a nasty witch who needed a good lesson in customer service, or did you think that maybe she blew out a tire on the way to work and got chewed out for being late? Are you judgmental, or are you compassionate?

Stephen Covey illustrates this concept in his book *The 7 Habits of Highly Effective People*: He (Covey) was riding the subway, hoping to enjoy a quiet ride. A father and his children got on the train, and the kids started making a terrible racket. Covey went to the father and admonished him to control his children's antics. The father looked up and said apologetically, "Oh, you're right. I guess I should do something about it. We just came from the hospital where their mother died about an hour ago. I don't know what to think, and I guess they don't know how to handle it either."

Covey had jumped to judgment, thinking only of the shattered peace he had hoped for, never considering that there might be a reason for the children's behavior.

It's so easy to judge, and so natural. But compassion feels so much better. Just experiment with compassion a little. Think of someone you judge and look at them through empathetic eyes. Do you see insecurity, self-doubt, fear? Could their actions be a desperate grasping for love, attention, and acceptance? If you realize that all dysfunctional behavior comes from an empty place that they are desperately trying to cover up, maybe you can see that it has less to do with you than you may have thought. The dysfunctional behavior you see on the outside is a reflection of the insecurity present on the inside.

A friend of mine works fifteen hours a day. He eats, sleeps, and breathes his job. But when you ask why he works so diligently, he will tell you that deep down he feels lazy, and he's afraid that someone will discover his secret shortcoming. He strives to compensate for something he feels, but no one sees.

Likewise, people who feel the most insecure about their looks are usually the best-looking. They always check the mirror or say how terrible their hair looks. Maybe they secretly fear that between glances at their reflection, their beauty will evaporate.

Very often people in positions of power are the most insecure about their power. Certain positions are imbued with authority; therefore we covet positions of importance because we think they give the people who fill them power. More than anyone, people in positions of power need our compassion because others' expectations of them are so high. They think they are supposed to know, be, or do it all. When they fall short, they often cover their failures with arrogance, dishonesty, or even misdirected blame.

It isn't always easy to have compassion for people who are in positions of power over us. We tend to think of them as having achieved something, or as having been given something we have not. Instead of thinking of your boss as a boss, think of her as a person. It's easier, and more productive, for two human beings to talk than it is for a boss and a subordinate to deliberate.

We tend to think of people who are famous, wealthy, or beautiful as having perfect, hassle-free lives. But celebrities face challenges in their relationships, just as you and I do. Actress, producer, and director Phylicia Rashad offers this perspective: "When people are difficult, or when we perceive them that way, they might be experiencing physical discomfort. They may not talk about it, or they're trying to deal with it and work through it in their own way. It's normal to be difficult when you're in pain and always pushing through physical obstacles." Ms. Rashad knew a person who was in pain, but he never talked about it. He was crabby, nasty, and always pushy. When he got over his physical problems, he was a different person. "Babies are like that," Ms. Rashad observes. "When a baby is wet, hungry, or lonely he cries out. He is uncooperative, demanding, and unpleasant. But change his diaper, feed him, or play with him, and his behavior changes dramatically."

While you're at it, be compassionate with yourself. Accept who you are and recognize that the bad parts of your personality are just a fraction of the total you. Work toward brightening those dark spots, instead of beating yourself up for not being perfect.

Door #8: The Closer We Get to Blame, the Further We Move from Solutions

You can't focus on two things at once. You're either blaming someone for a problem, or looking for a solution. What's it going to be? We live in a world that encourages blame, in a society where most people point fingers. Instead of accepting responsibility, people choose to find fault with others. Just look at the amount of lawsuits pursued in the United States.

Recently, I was at a copy center and the guy behind the counter showed me the copies that I'd requested. They were in the wrong order, stapled and collated. When I brought it to the clerk's attention, he showed me the originals that I'd given him. Lo and behold, they were in fact in the same wrong order as the copies. I was embarrassed, but I admitted my error. He thanked me for acknowledging my mistake and pointed out that most of the time customers blame the copy center for their own oversights.

We must take responsibility for our lives and our own role in how they run. Even when things happen to us that seem beyond our control, the very fact that we were present proves that we on some level influence events.

Door #9: Our Actions Create Our Reality

We think who we are determines how we act, but in fact how we act determines who we are. Change how you act and you become who you would like to be now. When you give someone a hug, it changes your physiological and emotional state. You become someone different in that moment.

If you don't like someone, treat him with kindness and respect anyway, and your thoughts of that person may change. This is why it is so important to do things for the sake of changing who you are in relation to others. Practice visualizing yourself in a positive exchange, think kind thoughts, and strive to improve your behavior. For instance, imagine yourself interacting with your hostile, explosive boss right now. You notice that your typical reaction is to cower, freeze from the intimidating moment, and agree to anything just to get out of there. Instead, replay the scene, but this time see yourself looking her in the eye, standing tall, and asking, "What's the next step we need to take to move this situation forward?" Imagining this will help you to feel and act stronger in her presence.

Door #10: Don't Take It Personally

Most of the time another person's difficultness isn't about you. When someone is difficult it is always a reflection of his innermost state. Even if you provoke or instigate his upset, it is not what you have done, but rather what you bring up in him. It may be something from the past that he still finds painful or chooses to ignore. Who knows what makes one person difficult at any particular time? One thing is certain: Everybody is somebody's difficult person at one time or another, including you. And the person you find most difficult may think exactly the same about you.

. . . And a Window: Have Patience

We're products of our environment. We steep in the marinade of a fast-paced world. Overnight delivery promised things sooner, but the immediacy of faxes and e-mail made overnight delivery seem slow. Technology has enabled us to do wonderful things, but it's also increased the tempo of life. We now expect everything to run at the speed of light. Relationships don't operate that way; they need time.

Don't think of difficult situations as some cosmic inevitability, or that things will never improve. Your relationships are like live organisms constantly changing and growing, and like all living things they need care, nurturing, and attention.

Ask couples that have been married for fifty years if their relationship is the same today as it was when they were courting. Invariably the answer will be no. You're a different person now than when you first opened this book. Every moment is dynamic while we are living, even if we aren't aware of it.

My hat is off to you for taking the first steps on this journey. Now that we have a clearer understanding of the principles involved, do you know why you react the way you do when confronted with difficult people? Why is it that the mere thought of them triggers emotional responses? They have you in an emotional headlock, but you aren't on the mat yet. Want to learn how to throw them off? Maybe the answer is as close as your own thoughts . . .

Thought into Action

ONE OF THE doors (or the window) will be a bigger issue for you than the others. When you've identified which area you need to work on the most, write it on a sticky note or index card and put it where you will see it every day. Focus on that particular statement, and make it part of your conscious thought. Notice that as you focus on it, you become connected to it. Note what you're learning and experiencing, and notice when resistance to the idea falls away. When you feel you have mastered one area, go on to another until all are so firmly entrenched in your thoughts that they guide your body language, your emotions, and your outlook.

THREE

Change Them, or Change Your Expectations?

The Heart of the Matter

Who is difficult? Sometimes it's a matter of chemistry. Have you ever felt that someone rubbed you the wrong way? Certain personality types may be inherently unappealing to you, or a person may do something in the first few seconds of your meeting that leaves you with a bad taste in your mouth. Then those first assessments go on to color whatever interactions will follow.

If you label people as difficult, then they are. Because of perceptions, someone you think of as difficult may seem like a saint to others. That may well be because your difficult person acts more negatively toward you than to others; but it could also be the glasses through which you see his or her behavior. To advance our understanding of this difficult person, we have to examine not just the difficult person's actions, but also our reactions to them. With that two-sided awareness, we can begin to change the observer that we are and see our challenges with that person in a new light.

Here's a simple definition: Difficult people are those who impede action. Their motivations may differ, and our opinions of them may vary, but they stand between us and our ability to make something happen, such as getting the report in on time, moving the project forward, or typing your letter without any mistakes.

Some people present inherent problems in particular situations (we'll explore those personality types in detail). They were born to be trouble, live to cause others trouble, and will probably die trouble. We perceive other people as being difficult because their agendas differ from ours. Whatever the cause, we can use speech, body language, and emotions to diffuse, dissolve, and disintegrate the barriers they throw up between us and our goals.

"Difficult" Is an Opinion

Everyone on your street agrees that Betty is a troublemaker. She doesn't pick up her overturned trash cans. She blares her polka records at 2 A.M. and she's never been on the business end of a pooper-scooper. When neighbors po-

litely ask her to be more respectful of the homeowners around her, she wags her finger, shouts obscenities, and commands Fido to chase them off the front porch.

Even though the consensus says that Betty is a difficult person, it's still an opinion. The neighbors share an assessment of Betty based on their observations and experiences with her. There may be other people who view Betty as considerate and respectful because of their observations and experiences with her.

Assessments and Assertions

Our eyes, ears, nose, mouth, and skin constantly collect information and relay it to the brain. These stimuli help us understand our environment and orient ourselves to our surroundings. With this information, we begin to evaluate the environment and make judgments about what we're processing. Our observations fall into two categories: assertions and assessments.

Assertions are quantifiable facts and can be observed: The sky is blue. That sweater is red. The room temperature is 78 degrees. Susie is 6 feet tall. Assessments, though, are the opinions we apply to our observations as they pass through our filters: "The sky looks lovely. That sweater is hideous. The room is hot. She's a big girl."

We are assessment machines. All day we make assessments about people, things, and situations. But assessments are dangerous, because once we make an assessment we accept it as fact. When we've made decisions about people, they become what we label them in our minds. These ideas harden until they become concrete, and we reinforce them until they trap us completely.

Assessments are the blocks to resolving our conflicts with difficult people, and not just because we label difficult people as horrible, mean, or rude. These assessments keep us pinned in a particular position, and in a particular relationship with difficult people, because they don't allow for a change in perspective. Once we identify our assessments and admit they are not fact, we are no longer as deeply bound by them.

What's Your Point of View?

If you're standing at the rim of the Grand Canyon, your assessment of it may be that it's vast and magnificent, but that it is basically a large hole surrounded by a lot of rock. From this perspective, you might assume that there's nothing of interest on the canyon floor, so you get back in the Airstream and drive away.

But if you'd moved beyond your preliminary assessment and journeyed to the bottom, you might have found an army of ants building the world's largest anthill, or a rock that captured your eye. Your devotion to your assessments may have kept you from witnessing some spectacular feat of nature.

In the same way our assessments can blind us. Sometimes our assessments can keep us from improving bad relationships or engaging in rewarding and productive ones. Assessments are so deeply embedded in our psyches that we don't see how they emerge, or how big a role they play in our thoughts and actions. If we're aware of how they form, and see them forming before we react to them, then we can use them to our benefit.

When Assessments Make Sense

It is important to understand the reasons for making assessments. In any situation ask yourself: Is this a fact (assertion) or an opinion (assessment)? Am I making a fair assessment based on objective standards? Is making this assessment benefitting me in some subtle way?

Let's say you think your co-worker is incompetent. You think so because she is slow in delivering assigned tasks. Are you assessing her fairly? Are you judging her performance or her personality? Or is it perhaps, on a deeper level, because assessing her as incompetent makes you look more competent? Perhaps you see your own shortcomings mirrored in her behavior. You don't like this about yourself, so you certainly won't tolerate it in her.

It is important to examine our assessments. Often we make assessments based more on ourselves and how someone compares to us, rather than on how the other person really measures up (to a predetermined standard).

In our co-worker example, the standards you use are based on your own ability to get the assignment done—or maybe your last assistant set the benchmark. To collect assertions that support your assessments, you might see how long it takes someone else to complete the same task. Now you have data. Maybe your co-worker does lack compentency, based on your measured standards. The advantage is that when your data supports the assessment you can provide solutions (such as training) instead of anger.

Believing Is Seeing

An old adage says that seeing is believing, but Brian Tracy, a popular personal enrichment teacher, says that believing is seeing.

Once you have made an assessment, you will look for things that support the assessment. Our evaluation of someone perpetuates itself as we look for proof to further validate the assessment, and discard evidence that is contrary or challenges the thought.

It is our need to be right that gets us in trouble. If we don't collect evidence, then we won't have to challenge our assessments. Is it so important to be right? Have you ever heard a boss make a comment like, "I knew Mary was going to blow this report!" What does the boss say when Mary does something wonderful? "Well, maybe Mary got the report done right this time, but she's always messing up." Mary's aptitude has been measured and declared below par, and now it's impossible for her to be seen in any other way. Her boss's assessment of Mary's abilities will never allow Mary to get ahead, nor will it allow the boss and Mary to establish a productive working relationship.

I once conducted an experiment, with interesting results. Try it yourself and see what happens for you. I sat on a park bench and watched people as they passed. I chose a man who was coming toward me, and I searched his face, his body, and his carriage for anything bad I could find. I saw that he was mean, rude, abrupt. I knew that if our eyes had met, and I'd have smiled or said hello, he would have grimaced or turned away sharply.

Then I looked at the same person for the good things I could see. Suddenly I saw that his eyes were kind, he held his head high, and there was a bounce in his step. When I looked for his goodness, I found it. Notice how what you look for will reveal itself to you. Become aware of how your assessments affect you personally as well as the people you come in contact with.

Assessments in Society

Assessments can be cultural, and so widely accepted that they aren't even questioned. Have you ever heard a mother proudly announce that her daughter is dating a doctor? What does that imply? That he's wealthy? Hard-working? Smart? Whether you have such concrete thoughts or not, you're still likely to find it impressive. If you're a woman whose daughter isn't dating a doctor, you might even be envious.

Shared assessments are also a factor in prejudice. But why are we so quick to size people up and categorize them? In a way, it's a social shorthand. We search for ways to make connections to others, or ways to protect ourselves from connecting with the "wrong" people. By making snap assessments based on factors such as social status, skin color, clothing style, occupation, or speech patterns, we eliminate a little bit of the work it takes to get to know someone. Or so we like to think.

When you give someone a label, you brace yourself for the way you think they're going to act. Your actions, therefore, stem from your assessments. Imagine how much our assessments of others ultimately determines our relationship with them. And vice versa.

Enough About Me, What Do You Think About Me?

Other people's negative assessments of us touch our own worst fears about ourselves. When a difficult person says, "You're a terrible person," they have in effect thrown open a window into the darkest recess of your own self-doubt, leaving you naked, vulnerable, and defensive.

Is your difficult person bothering you because he is critical and antagonistic, or because he is confirming your own feelings of inadequacy?

Whose Image Are You Living In?

When I was a child, my mother told me I was cold. I accepted that as a fact. If you had asked me to assess myself as I was growing up, I would have told you that I was cold. And having been identified as such, I couldn't act warm.

As an adult, I can see now that I do, in fact, have a cold side, but I also have a warm side. I've learned to embrace both of those things about myself, and to enjoy them both.

We act as though these assessments are properties of ourselves, as if you could cut me open and ice water would run out. We need to realize they're beliefs, and beliefs can be changed. Think about the ways you were labeled as a child: troublemaker, smart, funny, clumsy, and so on. In what ways do you still live that prophesy? In what ways does your difficult person label you in the same way you were labeled as a child?

Assessments in Context

Once we make assessments, they become like filters through which all of our encounters percolate. If you've decided that Kim is rude and doesn't like you, almost anything she says will sound like confirmation. Your assessment creates a context, you assume the context is reality, and whatever conversations take place within that context will be colored by it.

Our evaluations of others are based on a variety of factors: age, class, gender, race and skin pigment, spiritual orientation, energy level, sexual preference, education, and economic status.

Prejudices and preconceptions color how we relate to one another, and affect how our encounters will play out. For instance, if you don't like old people and I am 95 years old, there is already a barrier in our relationship. On the flip side, the person who is causing you difficulty may be doing so because she is applying her prejudices to you.

Prejudice is like static, interfering with our ability to

really see people as they are. So the first step to clearing your picture of your difficult person is to look in the mirror. Is it possible that you created distortions by applying your prejudices to him first? Have you made any judgment about him based on rumor, myth, or past experience? You may think that you're above that, but don't dismiss the possibility that you have treated this person, or responded to him, out of prejudice.

The following quiz will get you thinking about how you assess others.

Assessing Others

1. How quickly do I make assessments about people?

2. On what do I base my assessments?

3. How do my assessments influence the way I address my difficult person?

4. How does this person react to me as a result of how I have assessed and treated him or her?

5. Is there anything I would like to change about this? Do I have information that would allow me to rethink my initial impression of this person?

Now we know why we assess this person the way we do. But why is he or she like that? Why does he or she do the things that lead us to these assessments?

What Makes People Difficult?

The short answer is fear.

Whether difficult people act passively or aggressively, or swing between both, they are no doubt motivated by fear. They're insecure and lack confidence. They worry about having enough attention, recognition, and control.

Fear is a root that holds difficult people fast in their world. Their fear may cause them to be needy, self-indulgent, and unaware of what is going on around them. They may resist change, or insist on being right, knowledgeable, and victorious all the time.

Difficult people see themselves as victims, and they spend a lot of energy finding evidence to support that presumption. They think you don't understand them, and that may be one thing they're right about. But *they* don't understand either—not you, and not themselves. They see you as a component of the world that's so mean, and on some level, they may be right about that as well. Once you've engaged in the dance with them, you've become a part of their problems. And you may even encourage, reinforce, or feed their difficultness.

Understanding Fear

J. Krishnamurti, a philosopher, says, "Thought is responsible for fear; also thought is responsible for pleasure." We give so much power to fear that it disables us. But we don't give ourselves credit for the courage it takes to overcome fear. Fear traps everyone, not just difficult people, and knowing what you're afraid of is paramount to retraining your thinking.

Consider this information from Dennis Waitley's book *Seeds of Greatness*. He quotes a University of Michigan study that proved 60 percent of our fears are totally unfounded, 20 percent are fears of things that have already happened and are beyond our influence, and 10 percent concern minor matters that make little difference in our lives. Another 8 percent are "real and justifiable fears" but at least half of those are based on events we can't change. If we concentrated on the 2 percent of our fears that are real, and stopped dwelling on the rest, we could solve them easily. As Waitley puts it, "Stop stewing and start doing . . . knowledge and action."

Can your difficult person harm you? Harm your family? Fire you? Ruin your career? Cut you off from someone you love, or something you need? Keep you from having something you desire? Make you question your worth? What are you afraid will happen, and how does that fear reflect on your interactions with him or her? How valid are your fears?

These are good questions to be aware of. The answers may not be clear yet, but asking the questions opens doors to inner freedom and new perception.

Fear is like a blindfold against how things really are. This is also the fear we have of people who are different. We're so fearful of a particular group of people that we can't see the person in front of us.

Some of My Best Friends Are . . .

During the course of a seminar I happened to mention that I'm Jewish. At the end of the session, one of the participants approached me. "You're different. You're the first Jewish person I've met that I've liked."

What happened? Something about me shifted her concept of what Jewish people are like. She had lumped all Jewish people into a certain category, with certain characteristics, and judged them all to not be to her liking.

But I broke through her paradigm, and changed her thinking. Now maybe she can say, "Well, this person is different than I thought, and that person is different than I thought," and eventually she will see that if enough people don't fit into that mold, maybe there is something wrong with the mold.

How do you deal with an "ism"? One person at a time. Establish a relationship and be who you are. Use every opportunity to show that you're an individual. Maybe you do have some of the traits that are considered stereotypical of a group. But they are part of your makeup, and are also balanced out by a lot of other traits that are not.

Perhaps the little boy in the woods will think about his encounter with the sweet little dog later. Without the dog standing beside him, maybe he can see in his memory that the dog was loving and not at all scary. Maybe a tiny piece of his fear will chip away, and he can start to think that some dogs are good and some dogs are bad. We can all do the same with people.

Fear: Joy Killer

NOT TOO LONG ago, I was walking my neighbor's dog, a loving, enthusiastic Westie named Cody. A young boy and his dad were strolling along a nature trail when our paths crossed. The dog was friendly, and not threatening in any way. But because this boy is afraid of dogs, probably because he'd had a traumatic experience with one in the past, he couldn't see how safe and friendly this particular dog was. Cody wiggled up next to him and begged to be petted, but the boy reeled back in terror, unaware of the love in front of him, blinded by his own fear. He missed out on a great moment, and his perception of all dogs as vicious was reinforced.

Breakdowns

We often take the normal state of affairs for granted. People who live in San Diego say they don't even notice the lovely weather. But visitors are often overwhelmed by how beautiful everything is. "Wow, how does anybody go to work?" they wonder. "The sky is so blue, the air is so clear, the breeze is so warm!"

Natives become so accustomed to the weather and the scenery that it doesn't pierce their consciousness. The only time San Diegans seem to notice the weather is when it rains. By contrast, East Coasters complain bitterly about the hard winters, but they really appreciate the spring. Can you view the dark of night as a reason to appreciate the morning light? Can the bad moments make you aware of the times when you feel truly happy or serene? That which is transparent is very often unappreciated, and unnoticed. Anyone who's suffered a health problem will tell you how valuable good health really is.

Most of the time, we expect things to flow a certain way. We don't think much about the car we drive, the phone we talk on, or the computer we work on.

But what happens on a cold winter morning when the engine won't turn? When the phone goes dead? When the computer crashes? Interruptions are known as breakdowns, and we react to breakdowns in predictable ways. First, we get angry, curse, cry, panic, and fume. Then we see past the emotional crisis, and act to overcome the breakdown. Call the tow truck, ask a neighbor to report the phone problem, or find a computer technician.

Breakdowns cause stress and anxiety because they interrupt our ability to get something done. Who will pick up your kids if you can't get the car started? How will you reach your clients without a phone? When will your reports get out if you can't use your computer? Sometimes the solutions come easily—another carpool driver can make sure the kids won't be stranded—but other times the breakdowns have deeper implications, and the resolutions are more complex. Life is not so much about the breakdowns we encounter, but about how we deal with them.

Difficult people cause breakdowns for us. They stall our creativity, cut off our communications, and interfere with our ability to process information. People breakdowns are more frustrating. A car doesn't care if you change its battery or rewire its electrical system, but people will resist, and probably resent, your attempts to "fix" them.

Just as you would enlist the services of an auto mechanic or a computer technician, you may need help with your people breakdowns. It probably won't do much for your relationship to tell your difficult person, "You're broken and you need therapy." So again, the place to fix the glitch is not at its source, but within yourself. You cannot force the car to get moving and get the kids, but you can find another route around the problem. By the same token, you can't force difficult people to change, but you can find another route around them.

So how do you deal with your people breakdowns? Your answers to the following quiz will give you an idea of how you react to situations with difficult people, and will provide the first key to understanding your role in these exchanges.

How Does This Person Affect Me?

YES or NO?

_____   *I feel drained after speaking to this individual.*

_____   *My mood sours after contact with him or her.*

_____ *My self-esteem diminishes during our interactions.*

_____ *My muscles tense and my teeth clench when this person is around.*

_____ *I feel an urge to flee.*

_____ *I'm relieved when this person is gone.*

_____ *I fantasize about him or her suffering.*

_____ *I'd throw a party if I discovered I didn't have to see this person again.*

_____ *I plan ways to avoid him or her.*

_____ *This person brings out the worst in me. I act differently with him or her than I do with other people.*

If you answered yes to more than two questions, then you are somewhat affected by this person; more than four yes answers means you are very affected; and more than six means that you may need help. High levels of stress can cause headaches, nausea, digestive disorders, and long-term health problems.

In your darkest moments, there may seem to be no hope for untangling the web in which a difficult person has ensnared you. But there are ways to separate the threads and break free. The place to start is where you are trapped: at the very center, inside yourself.

Thought into Action

THINK ABOUT THE assessments you have about yourself in different domains. What do you think about yourself as an employee or worker? Parent? Financial manager? Friend? For example, you might see yourself as a hard worker, a concerned and dedicated parent, a frugal money manager, or loyal friend. Write them down in your journal. On what assertions, what factual elements, do you base these opinions? When did you decide to claim these characteristics? Are these assessments primarily positive or negative? How many of your negative assessments have no factual basis? How long have you been harboring negative assessments about yourself that you made up? What will it take to change them?

Take a moment to examine your self-assessments. What negative assessments are you harboring that you can free yourself from? Have any of your assessments changed over time?

FOUR

Why Me? Why Them?

In his book *From the Finite to the Infinite*, the Indian saint Swami Muktananda says, "Man has taken birth to attain love, to jump with love, to dance with love, and to swim in the ocean of love. He didn't take birth to fight with others, to be confused, to have conflicts . . ."

So how do we move from conflict and into love? Believe it or not, asking "Why me?" will lead you there. Examining why this is happening to you—not from a place of victimization, but from a place of learning—will provide understanding on a deeper level, help you cope, and ultimately transform the way you view the situation.

Why Is It You?

"Why me?" you ask. "If the other person is causing me difficulty, why do I have to examine myself to find the solutions?" Freedom.

You can free yourself from the pain, the suffering, the

manipulation, and the disappointment. You're the one who is chafing. Your goals are being blocked. And since it's not at all possible to change the behavior of another person, or force him or her to see the world differently, you must concentrate on the only thing you have the power to change—yourself.

Real change is not without some discomfort. Facing difficult people is tough, but not dealing with them will lead to greater problems in the long run. It's easy to want to change. It's harder to do it. The good news is that discipline leads to wisdom. Use what you're discovering about yourself and others to your benefit. Difficult people don't operate in a vacuum. In fact, their actions aren't even a problem until they cause a problem for you. Realize that their arrows only do harm when they hit a target. Then you can stop being a target.

A Hollow Victory

A few years ago, I was preparing a seminar for a client. He told me his secretary would copy my handouts, but he warned me that she was a procrastinator. I called a week ahead to get the process started. She was busy that day, so she asked me to call back on Wednesday; on Wednesday she put me off until Friday.

I was irritated but I took a deep breath and agreed to call again. Before Friday rolled around, I sent her the materials so she could jump into action after our conversation.

Friday came and, in her desperation, she promised me

that she would have everything ready if I could pick it up Sunday afternoon. Despite the inconvenience, and my mounting impatience, I agreed.

On Sunday I showed up, but she did not. I waited for hours, and gave up at dinnertime. I made the hour-long trip back home, and just as I turned the key in my front door, the phone rang. "Your material is ready," she said, "can you come pick it up now?"

My frustration and anger flared, and my temper got the better of me. The conversation that followed went something like this:

"How dare you?" I bellowed. "You made me wait all day and you have the nerve to call me now?"

"How dare *you*?" she bellowed back. "I've taken my Sunday afternoon to get you these materials and this is how you show your appreciation? How can you talk to me that way?"

"You don't have to worry about how I talk to you anymore!" I wailed, and—click—down went the phone.

For a moment I felt victorious. Then I realized she had my originals.

I had to do some repair work. As hard as it was, I called back and said, "I'm sorry." She was too. Then we made arrangements to exchange the materials.

I had become as much a part of the problem as she was. I had to take responsibility for my role in the conflict. What I'd done wrong was to let the week pass without expressing my frustration and my need to have the materials ready before the seminar. What I hadn't done was

pin down a specific time to meet. So while I felt very righteous about my anger, she saw my behavior as irrational
and out of proportion. And when I launched my attack,
her reaction was to strike back. I realized then that people
don't care why you are angry, just *that* you are angry.
They pay attention to the emotion and not the reason behind it. Taking responsibility for my emotion diffused her
and solved the problem.

Not That Again!

In my years of giving seminars and workshops, I have
heard the laments of hundreds of people in business, government, and associations, and detailed accounts of the
horrors difficult people visit upon them. While every case
is unique, some patterns still emerge.

Some difficult people talk too much, others not enough.
Some are loud, overbearing, and physically or verbally
abusive. Some are tyrants; others are indecisive. Some nag,
whine, and complain; others are explosive. Some lie, some
sabotage relationships, some simply lack integrity. Are
you a victim? Wonder why? The answer is simple: These
are all coping mechanisms that have worked for difficult
people to some degree, and now they are working on you.
And while you may not see or understand the rewards,
they're present nonetheless. People wouldn't repeat their
actions if there weren't benefits.

What do difficult people gain? They get their way. They
intimidate others into going along with them. Some people

find sport in making others angry or upset or intimidated. Some feel a sense of power and control when they can negatively affect someone else.

How does your difficult person upset you? Look at it as objectively as possible. Rather than labeling her as rude, pinpoint what she does that makes her rude. Does she interrupt you, curse at you, ignore you, or laugh at you? How do you define rudeness? Look at what she says, how she says it, what signals her body language sends even when her tongue is still. What is the emotional flavor of your conversations? Are they taut, sarcastic, unproductive?

The Trap of the Status Quo

By justifying the way we deal with difficult people, we are choosing to plow ahead as before, butting heads and living in conflict. We've convinced ourselves that the other person is wrong, and we can offer proof. Sometimes just thinking about the person who is causing so much friction evokes the emotions and bodily responses we actually experience in his or her presence.

What's the difference between an emotion and a mood? How do the two affect one another? What are these moods and emotions that we experience, either in this person's presence or in our head? When you become aware of these moods and emotions, you can change them as if you were shifting the gears in your car.

FIVE

How to Change Your Mood—
and Theirs

*All emotions have their place. There are times, for ex-
ample, when we each need to feel angry or sad—because that is the inner truth we are experiencing right
then. And there are times when it is right to feel anxious, concerned, joyful or jealous. Unlike the mind,
the heart finds it difficult to lie.*

—*Robert K. Cooper and Ayman Sawaf,* Executive EQ

Moods and Emotions

Moods are states of being. They are where we live.
Emotions explode suddenly, and are dictated, or at least
influenced, by the mood. By changing your mood, you can
alter the emotional responses you have to the same circumstances.

Sometimes, you can be in such a bad mood that nothing

can pick you up. Anything that happens reinforces your zone. A friend can even send you flowers, and you'll think, "I don't deserve flowers." Luckily, good moods are equally persistent. If you're feeling like a million bucks and something unfortunate happens, you would probably say, "That's okay, I can deal with it. Today nothing can bring me down."

Events don't necessarily define the emotions that get triggered. But moods create a framework or context for your responses. You're walking down the street and you see a snake. You gasp, panic, recoil. But in another instance you may be out on a nature trail, looking for something interesting. The same snake crosses your path, but this time you think: "Cool, I saw a snake."

What mood do you live in? What moods do you see around you? How does your difficult person perceive life? The mood or state you live in influences how you deal with situations as they arise. Does your mood allow you to take crises in stride, or does it exaggerate them?

Moods and behavior are related, and understanding that relationship can help us reverse unproductive behavior. For instance, nutrition experts encourage dieters to examine the way they feel when they overeat or choose high-calorie foods. Some people lose control of their eating habits if they're depressed or stressed. But they can learn other ways of relieving those emotions; the mood doesn't have to dictate the response.

Figure out how your behavior is associated with a mood, and realize that the two aren't intrinsically connected. You behave a certain way at work because of the mood you're in at work, and your behavior is a habitual manifestation of the mood. We've seen that bad habits can be changed or replaced with more productive ones.

A mood is like a cup. If you have a good frame of mind, the cup is empty, and can accommodate droplets of water that drip into it. If you live in a negative mind-set, the cup is already full. Drips overwhelm the cup and make you overflow. If you find a way to be more positive you lower the level of frustration you carry around with you. You don't have to spend your life being a slave to your mood. Changing your mood will allow you to absorb more. Do your difficult people really cause your bad mood, or are you so full of bad feelings that they are spilling you over? If your mood isn't one that you want to live in, it's time to make a change. How do you change a mood? Later in this chapter we discuss nine external and three internal methods for changing a bad mood, but here are three immediate ways: (1) Find someone living in a mood you want to be in. (2) Ask this person how he or she thinks and what he or she thinks about. (3) Find something to be happy about every day.

Within two years, Lucy's father and her six-year-old daughter died. These losses were terribly painful and she grieved for them both, but they didn't devastate her. Because she lives in a generally upbeat mood and has an overall positive attitude, she was able to be strong and carry on. Lucy thinks some people have an inborn optimism that pulls them through. The moods we live in de-

Frank and Ernest

© 1996 Thaves/Reprinted with permission. Newspaper dist by NEA, Inc.

termine how we handle adversity—and that includes how we handle difficult people.

Moods are also cultural. Washington, D.C., has a more conservative mood than California. And people living in war-torn countries have a different mood from those living in a prosperous, peaceful nation.

Cultural moods exist within workplaces and families, too. What is the cultural climate where you live and work? Can you leave a negative environment? Can you have a better mood and still exist in that environment? If you can't leave it, could you try insulating yourself and not letting the moods of others infect your own? Start by choosing your company more carefully. Whiners and complainers are looking for allies. Don't allow yourself to be poisoned by their toxic attitude. Remind yourself that joining them in their misery will corrupt your state of mind.

One company had such bad morale that the employees would bet at the beginning of each month how many would quit within the following four weeks. Conversations around the water cooler concerned who was having what problem with whom. Very little productive work took place, and discontent spread through the ranks like wildfire. Those who were truly unhappy left. Those who stayed just enjoyed the gossip and the friendships that formed against the common enemy—the managers.

The place where you experience the problem is the place where the problem needs to be addressed—first. You can do other things to improve relationships, but there is nothing out there that doesn't exist within you. Good or bad, every experience you have has something to do with you.

The Good Old Days?

In hindsight, moods can change, or our memory of them can change. Remember the 1950s? The happy days? Everyone was happy, all the time. Except for African Americans, and housewives, and probably lots of other people.

We romanticize relationships in this way too. When the time comes to end a relationship, or after it has ended, we tend to forget the bad times and the bad emotions and hold the high points as greater than they were.

Many people live in a state of discontent or despair. Discontent is expressed by the statement, "I hate what happened." Despair is negative anticipation about what's to come: "Nothing good is ever going to happen. It's hopeless."

You can live in these two extremes or you can accept. Acceptance brings you to peace. Acceptance is alignment with reality and allows for hopefulness, anticipation, and excitement about the future. If you accept your difficult situation, you may not be changing it but rather your relationship to it. When you change your relationship to it, you won't feel the need to change it anymore.

While we can change our perspective, the fact is that conflict occurs in relationships. How we handle the conflict is a reflection of our commitment to the relationship. One measure for determining that commitment to the relationship is our emotional bank account, illustrated in the following example.

Your Emotional Bank Account

Libby, who is in the advertising specialty business, was having T-shirts made for a charitable event given by one of her clients. As a favor to her client, Libby charged a rock-bottom price, making almost no profit herself. She called her favorite silkscreener for the printing of the shirts.

The mill from which Libby was buying the T-shirts was in the same town as the silkscreener. She asked the mill to give her an estimate for shipping the goods back to her client. After her client approved the charges (including shipping), she requested that the silkscreener double-check the shipping costs. The silkscreener told her that everything was fine with the order and proceeded to print the shirts. The shirts were delivered and the client was thrilled, but when Libby got the bill, the shipping costs were more than double the estimate the mill had given her. It turns out that the silkscreener had used a different shipper whose costs were higher. While Libby recognized what the problem was, she felt that it was the silkscreener's responsibility to alert her to the discrepancy. When she approached the silkscreener with the situation, the silkscreener became defensive. Libby realized that the silkscreener did not want to acknowledge her responsibility. Since there was little profit to begin with, Libby was in a bind.

Libby said, "In my assessment, it was your responsibility to confirm the shipping costs that I had been given by the mill to make sure they were correct." The silkscreener then threw up a barrier. She said that the shipping costs weren't her problem, repeatedly explained her point of view, insisted that she did nothing wrong, and interrupted Libby when she tried to explain.

Libby quickly sized up her opponent. She knew that the silkscreener's pride in the moment blocked her from taking responsibility. Because of that she didn't make it about who was right or wrong, she made the issue the relationship. Libby used verbal aikido (see p. 173) to diffuse her. She said, "We've been through a lot of obstacles over the years. We've jumped through many hoops for our clients. Through it all, you've always come through for me. I've really appreciated our relationship and I don't want to fight about this. This isn't just about money, it's about our relationship. Why don't you take a little time to think about it, and then see what you feel like doing."

Libby's words had opened a door to a solution. About a week later, the silkscreener called back with an offer of vouchers for the difference in shipping charges so that Libby would ultimately be reimbursed and the silkscreener wouldn't lose a customer.

Now you might wonder what Libby should have done if the silkscreener had refused to pay, or why she didn't get an estimate in writing. In Libby's business, transactions move quickly and often there isn't time for written estimates, although that might have been a better solution. If the silkscreener had refused to pay, Libby would have had to pay for the charges and perhaps would never have done business with the silkscreener again. But in this circumstance she created a win for both parties.

The key is to ask "What's possible?" instead of "Whodunit?" and take the conversation into the future instead of rehashing the past. Breakdowns don't happen in a vacuum, and in Libby's case it happened in the context of a good, long-standing relationship. There was a precedent set, a mutual respect and foundation of warm feelings. It's as though the women had an emotional bank account, and had racked up credit with one another that allowed for a certain amount of negativity before it bankrupted the friendship. Had the problem occurred between two strangers, the actions, reactions, and outcome would have been different. They wouldn't have had anything invested, would have been off to a bad start, and would have had no reason to work toward a resolution.

What Libby did was brilliant. She didn't say, "Don't

do that." That's like two hard objects crashing against one another. Instead she remained calm and said, "Let's work this out," and then put it back into the other woman's hands. By working out their differences, they were able to replenish their emotional bank account and continue their working relationship.

Building emotional bank accounts is important, but it's also important to know when you've bankrupted your own. You can tell someone, "I'm exhausted right now and I can't deal with this." Know your limits, and don't try to function in the market when your pockets are empty.

Recognize that other people have limits, too. When they're too drained to deal with you, or act when they should be retreating, have compassion and don't take it personally. Watch for people being short with you, reacting emotionally, and not treating you with respect. When you see that happening, back off.

Is your difficult person really snapping at what you've done? Or did twenty other problems precede you? Try saying this: "I heard your phone ringing all morning and I can see that you're under a lot of pressure. Maybe we can plan to talk about this when things quiet down." Take some of that external pressure off both of you.

Programmed for Success

As a programming supervisor for an organization, Allen oversees Ella. Her job is to plan a particular course, book a meeting room, find the speakers, and register the attendees. But it takes her forever to get the job done, and she calls him to complain about why things aren't progressing or why she has to exceed her budget.

Ella was becoming a difficult person for Allen. But he decided to see her as a teacher, and to use his experience with her to learn from it. When she finally got some arrangements made, he praised her to the heavens. He offered her the most positive feelings he possibly could, and she was very happy when she hung up the phone.

Every time he deals with Ella, he emphasizes the good things, and minimizes the bad. He's building up his emotional bank account with her. If something goes wrong in the future, they will have this built-up bond from which they can draw.

As in this case, sometimes the solution is changing your behavior so much that the other person's behavior changes in turn. By doing this you never get to the point of having to discuss his or her shortcomings.

So how do you determine what to do in any situation? Do you avoid dealing directly with other people's shortcomings, or only modify your own behavior or reactions? You basically have three options. These choices are outlined in what I call the *BOP method* for dealing with the difficults.

BOP the Problem

Using the BOP method for resolving conflicts doesn't mean you carry a Louisville slugger in your backpack and bop someone in the head the moment they cause you stress. It's a set of options you can exercise when faced with a difficult person. Each option applies to a different set of circumstances, and the level of effort is in proportion to the stakes involved in maintaining the relationship.

Here are the three components of this method:

Be compliant. Just go along, accept the situation, and don't do anything to change the outcome. This is most appropriate when the stakes are low, and you have little or no interest in continuing your relationship with the difficult person.

Operate from the opposite. Identify what response the person wants from you, and do the opposite. If she wants attention, ignore her. If she is trying to get you angry, laugh. As with the first approach, this is most effective in low-stakes situations, and it won't go very far toward building a lasting friendship.

Practice carefrontation. When you confront someone your stance is one of opposition. But if you carefront your difficult person, you assume a posture of unity. Then his defenses aren't necessary, and you can have a productive dialogue.

There are three steps to carefrontation.

1. Get him in a place where you can talk to him alone. Don't attempt this conversation in the middle of a staff meeting or in the elevator.

2. Get his permission. A simple question like "Can we talk?" gives him the chance to say, "No, I'm sorry, I'm on my way out." Then you can make arrangements to talk another time. If you blurt out your issues, you may detect impatience, or feel rudely cut off when he runs from the office. It also helps prepare him; if he sees it coming and doesn't feel like he's been ambushed, he's more likely to listen to your concerns. And in the final analysis, what you're really asking for is his attention. His response will tell you if you are going to get it.

3. Tell him your assessment of the situation, and be careful to put it in those terms. "The way I see it . . ." "It seems to me . . ." "I'm getting the impression . . ." This is much more effective than accusations like "You always . . ." "You never . . ." "I hate when you . . ." Then, give him the opportunity to respond. Ask, "Do you share the same perception?" or "Do we really have a problem?" His response might be, "You are the problem." Or he might say, "Wow, I had no idea this was bothering you." Carefrontation lays the cards on the table and reviews both players' opinion of the hand. The discussion might not solve the problem, but it can bring you closer to solving it.

Carefrontation requires a lot of emotional energy—and in some cases a bit of risk—so I recommend it when the

A Time-Out for Mom

I KNOW A mother of two small boys. She works at home, and sometimes the children demand attention at exactly the same moments she needs to be making phone calls, doing research, or writing.

She noticed she was getting frustrated and angry with the kids, especially when they asked for stories or a game and didn't comply when she pleaded for their patience. Their demands escalated, she became more frustrated, and then she'd blow up at them. When she calmed down, she felt guilty for being so cross with her children, and upset with herself for doing such a poor job balancing the two.

But then she realized that sometimes she really enjoyed reading, playing cards, and chasing her kids around the house, the very same things that irritated her when she was trying to work. The things the children were doing were not causing her emotions to be negative, but rather the mood she was in was causing her to react negatively. When she was working, her mood was one of stress and anxiety.

She made a deliberate decision to relax around the children, put aside her work to give them a dose of affection, and recognize that the moments she was able to share with them were far too precious to infect with hostility. They are her gift, and she finally understood that it is within her power to enjoy her time with them. All she had to do was change her mood.

stakes are high, for people who need to work together or maintain a long-term relationship.

The BOP method is a very deliberate way to change your mood or emotion. Sometimes changing your mood requires a lot of focus and thought—but sometimes you can find your source of relief right in front of you.

Mood Changers

How do we change our moods? We can take two routes to arrive at a new mood: external and internal. Here are nine external and three internal mood changers. Some you can do right at your desk, while others will be reserved for downtime.

External Mood Changer #1: Call or See Someone Who Makes You Feel Good

As we know, the stronger of two emotions will dominate. Find someone who is sunny and positive. Surrender yourself to another person and bluntly ask for help, or simply bask in his or her presence. Allow this person to influence you in a positive way.

Some people are inherently good-natured and optimistic, and they tend to attract others like them. Andrea says Kelly is one of those people. She has boundless energy and a gentle, kind heart. People learn a lot from her about what it means to be a friend. The surprise came at Kelly's anniversary party, when Andrea met a roomful of Kelly's lifelong friends. She was struck by the way everyone in Kelly's circle had that same radiance and warmth. What are your friends like?

The flip side is to get away from people that bring you down, and recognize that people who share your perspective will be drawn to you.

I recently ran into a guy I'd dated years ago. When I asked him how he was doing, he complained about all the bad things that were happening in his life. I wasn't surprised by his answer, because he'd always complained about his life.

What did surprise me was that I couldn't remember why I'd ever been attracted to this person. He was so negative. I wondered if he'd become more so since the last time I'd seen him, but then I realized he hadn't really changed that much.

But I had changed. When we were together, I was also very unhappy, and spent a lot of time grousing about this thing or that. Now that I was more positive, I couldn't connect with him.

External Mood Changer #2: Shut Up and Listen

Use music to uplift and soothe you, and to create an atmosphere that lightens your mood. A familiar song can evoke memories of pleasant times and good feelings. And different kinds of music can help you create different moods.

If singing helps, belt it out. Tote along CDs in your car that have a calming effect. You can choose what you hear, avoid annoying commercials, and replay your favorite selections. And if you don't already love classical music, give it a try. You'll find that the works of the masters have the ability to touch the deepest chords of human emotion.

External Mood Changer #3: Look Outward

See an amusing or inspiring movie. Go to a café or a party and watch people. Do something nice for someone else—anything that will distract you from focusing on yourself.

The other day I visited a friend who was critically ill. She was so happy that I'd come to see her. But I was the one who had received a gift—of appreciation, gratitude, and love. How could I feel discouraged about my life when a dying woman could find happiness in the mere presence of another human being? It turned out to be the last time I saw her.

To open your heart it helps to give something of yourself. Work in a food bank. Deliver meals to the homebound. Shovel an elderly woman's sidewalk. Another's misfortune can help us keep our own problems in perspective. When you truly serve someone else, it serves you infinitely more.

External Mood Changer #4: Eat a Piece of Chocolate (But Not the Whole Box!)

Chocolate releases an endorphin called serotonin, the brain's natural chemical upper. Endorphins are believed to be responsible for the pleasant physical sensations we feel when we are in love, and for the body's ability to tolerate or overcome pain.

The trick is to slow down enough to really enjoy the taste. Let your tongue experience all of the notes and flavors of the chocolate, and tune in to the endorphin surge. Have one or two, but don't gorge on the whole box. That will leave you feeling guilty and out of control.

External Mood Changer #5: Exercise

Another way to raise your endorphin level is to exercise. And exercise offers other mood-lifting benefits: It relieves stress, gets you out of the environment that may be the site of your conflicts, distracts you from your problems, and strengthens your body.

Unfortunately this requires more of a commitment, and may not be the quick fix chocolate is. But the long-term rewards are worth it.

If you are sitting at a desk, try this mini exercise to keep your body flexible. Simply rock your pelvis forward and back. Go ahead. Wiggle. What happens to your spine? It follows the pelvis. Rock and roll. By doing this small movement a few times an hour, you can keep your neck more relaxed, keep your spine flexible, and shortcut potential back pain. Much of the pain we get in our bodies is from not moving, so make sure you get up or get down!

External Mood Changer #6: Get a Massage

Massage will relax your muscles, soothe aches and knots, and make you feel pampered. If you're at your desk, do self-massage to remind your muscles you haven't forgotten about them.

External Mood Changer #7: Collect Toys

Buy mind toys and keep them at your desk. Something as simple as a Slinky, a wind-up doll, or balls to juggle will distract your overworked mind for a few moments, and give your body a break from sitting in the same position. If that feels too silly for you, try something to lighten up your desk, like a joke-a-day calendar. If today's doesn't make you chuckle, move ahead.

External Mood Changer #8: Collect Pictures

Keep a picture of someone you love close to you during the day. When you're feeling overwhelmed, look at the picture and talk to the person in it. What would you say to this person? What would he or she say to you? (Note: It is best not to do this one out loud in a busy office. People will wonder.)

External Mood Changer #9: Find a Child, Dog, or Cat

Children are innocent, their thoughts are pure, and they revel in their natural wonder about the world. They don't yet understand how to be manipulative, dishonest, cagey, or self-defeating. Just being around them for a few moments may awaken the purity and childlike joy that lies dormant within you. Let them invite you to play.

Studies show that animals also have a soothing effect. If nothing else, being around kids or pets takes you outside yourself, if only for a moment.

Internal Mood Changer #1: Target the Root Cause. Ask Yourself, "Why Am I Really Upset?"

This is especially important if your response is out of proportion, or inappropriate for the situation. So look for the issue behind the issue, the root cause for your mood. Are you upset because your husband left the cap off the toothpaste, or because he lost his job four years ago and watches TV instead of looking for a new job?

Underlying causes can cast shadows in unlikely places, and those basic problems are rarely discussed. Maybe you fly off the handle because Brenda gave you a report ten minutes late. Assuming the delay didn't have bad consequences for you, this response is out of proportion. Are you angry because Brenda didn't invite you to her Christmas party? Maybe you think it's too petty to discuss with her, but you feel hurt nevertheless. Maybe you're trying to show her that she's made you unhappy, even if you do it underhandedly.

Internal Mood Changer #2: Get What You Need

Once you've identified what the real problem is, ask yourself what you need to do to fix it. What do you need right now, and how can you get it? Are you hungry? Tired? Are you overbooked? Can you delegate responsibilities to someone else? If you are tired and drained but sleeping is out of the question, maybe you can close your eyes for a few minutes of power napping. Or cancel your dinner plans so that at least you can look forward to rest at the end of the day. Plan a break for yourself. Turn down requests or invitations that will tire you even more. Maybe you just need to do nothing.

Internal Mood Changer #3: Be Quiet and Breathe

Find peace in solitude. Carve out fifteen minutes of the day for quiet time. Batteries that grow weak strengthen after time on a charger. You can recharge too. Meditate. Take a catnap. Breathe deeply. Stare at a picture of a tranquil forest trail and imagine yourself there. If fifteen minutes is too much, close your eyes for five minutes. As much as 75 percent of our stress comes from just having our eyes open, so shut them! Giving your eyes a rest will give *you* one. Find a way to do this every day (not recommended while driving).

Anger

What to Do with Another's Anger

Swami Muktananda writes in *From the Finite to the Infinite*, "Look for the source of anger.... When a person's desire is not fulfilled, it turns into anger. When a person gets really angry, he wants to hurt someone, and when this happens he loses his discrimination. If a person loses his discrimination, understand that he is destroying himself."

An angry person doesn't want to be questioned by the target of her anger. She wants to be heard. Anger usually has two components: the root cause of distress, and the exacerbating helplessness when no one listens. So listen to an angry person. Don't try to calm him, or tell him he isn't entitled to his anger. Listening transforms anger, and once he feels like you're paying attention, you can explore the source of the problem. Whether or not a person's anger is justified, it still exists, and its very existence needs to be dealt with.

If someone approaches you in anger, pull it out and move it through. Give her the opportunity to vent it. Don't trivialize it, but don't overvalidate it either. Say, "I can see that you're angry." Recognizing her anger and letting it flow will reduce its intensity, and give you some very valuable information about her perception of your actions. This is when you get to find out what he thinks you have "done wrong."

Listen carefully. As you listen, stay neutral and don't take it personally. Very often what makes the person angry is not that something is amiss, but that her irritation is not being given the proper attention. If someone takes a moment to listen to her, to let her vent, she'll be so surprised that her anger will dissolve. Meanwhile, while you are dealing with this person, count to ten inside. Remember that people often regret the words they use in anger. Ask yourself, "How will I feel about myself later if I act out now?" Remember to breathe. It changes the intensity of the moment for you. Let this be about the other person. Don't take in her anger.

Recently I attended a retreat where I saw a man approach a hotel employee in the reception area, fuming about his accommodations. Rather than get defensive or quickly patch things up, she brought him a glass of water and sat down to listen to his concerns. His anger blew forth like a hot wind, and then he fell silent. She gave him her attention, stopped him from escalating into yet more fury, and validated his position. She let him know that his feelings were important.

Some people are convinced that anger is a normal way to be noticed, and they use it regularly. One way to recognize this pattern is when you see anger that is over-dramatized, irrational, or used repeatedly. Such people make others afraid of angering them, and they use that

Check with Me

SUSAN AND JOHN were friendly business associates, and they often did favors for one another. When John's company was having accounting problems, he asked Susan to pick up his mail and deposit any checks that arrived into her own account. It was February, and he told her he wouldn't need the money until the end of the year.

What started out as a commitment to take some envelopes out of her mailbox soon turned into a complicated bookkeeping procedure, but she stuck with it because she'd agreed to help out. When John ran short on cash in May, he asked Susan for the money. She'd thought he wouldn't want it for a while, so she'd taken the money out and used it for other things. She knew that she'd have no problem replenishing it by the end of the year, but in the spring it wasn't there.

He was furious. "That was my money!" he shouted. "How could you use it?" Susan was frustrated by the misunderstanding. Besides, she was doing him a favor! "How dare you get angry at me?" she demanded. "All of a sudden you've changed your mind and now you're upset? And after all I've done for you!"

He accused her of not keeping good records, and then insisted she repay him right away. As she listened to his tirade, she realized he wasn't going to recognize her frustration about the situation. He was only concerned about getting his money. How this task, and his anger, affected her was of no interest. He needed to vent.

Susan realized John needed an audience for his anger. Her angry response wouldn't be productive or lead to a satisfactory solution. When she backed down, he started to calm. When his fire was spent, they were able to talk rationally about what happened and what had to happen next to make them both happy. The situation resolved quickly after that as he was able to hear Susan's concerns. He agreed to never make such a request in the future and she agreed to get him the money within two weeks.

fear to influence and control others. Ignore people like this. It may make them more angry in the short term, but eventually they will see that this tactic does not win them the attention they seek.

What to Do with Your Own Anger

Friedrich Nietzsche wrote that recovering from wounds makes us tremendously powerful. Can you look at others' trespasses against you that way? If someone has done something to anger you, view those wounds as opportunities for growth.

Would you rather be angry or great? Would you rather be right or happy? The need to be right makes us defensive and acts as a barrier between us and our own happiness. Let your difficult person be "right" (whatever that means) if that makes you happy by relieving your stress. If it doesn't, then remember to deal with the situation and not the person. The more you focus on him, the more he pulls you in. Talk to him in terms of solution to the situation and move on as quickly as possible. If it escalates then walk away. Refuse to play his game.

By allowing him to be right, you free yourself from the struggle. When winning is no longer important, the battle ceases to be necessary.

The authors of *Executive EQ*, Robert K. Cooper and Ayman Sawaf, offer a three-step strategy for channeling your own emotional energy. First, don't deny or minimize the intense sensations. Allow yourself to feel the emotion, and acknowledge its presence. Second, listen to the information the emotion is sending you. What is at stake? Which of your values or goals are being challenged? And third, guide or channel the energy into an "appropriate, constructive response."

Ways to Deal with Your Own Anger

1. *Physically.* Get a tennis racquet and hit a pillow. Work out. Break something. I once broke all the dishes in my cabinet. It was a mess, but I felt good.

2. *Mentally.* Talk out your anger, with a confidant or with yourself. Ask yourself, "How is holding on to this anger serving me? Do I want to stay in this state?"

3. *Emotionally.* Underneath anger is pain, underneath pain are tears. Have a good cry.

4. *Spiritually.* Seek guidance from a higher power. If you believe in God, pray for help. Ask that your anger be lifted, or imagine that your anger is like a lump of dough that you heave out into space. See your anger as something outside of you. Ask God to take it from you.

In his book *The Healer Within*, Roger Jahnke demonstrates the power of redirecting anger by relating an anecdote from Maria, a therapist at UCLA. Her patient had an uncontrollable urge to hit. He was documented as having a hundred episodes a month of hitting, at times violently. She taught him to deepen his breath, relax, and make specific movements with his hands that coincided with his breathing. In a short time, he began to gain control of these urges. He was able to redirect his internal impulses by using the breath and the body. Within eight weeks he had reduced the number of hitting episodes to fewer then fifteen. Ultimately he was able to prevent them altogether.

By working on redirecting your anger response and letting the angry person vent, you will clear the air for a rational, productive discussion.

Learning to Let Go

Pride and anger go hand in hand. Righteous indignation swells when you feel you've suffered an injustice, and you're entitled to be angry. However, it would be better to swallow your pride and let it go—especially if you realize that being angry won't produce a change.

In her book *Molecules of Emotion*, Dr. Candace Pert tells a story of how she learned to let go of the most important fight of her career. She had found a drug, Peptide T, that she thought could cure AIDS, but she couldn't get funding for drug testing. She went to one of Deepak Chopra's seminars and as an audience member asked, "Deepak, I don't know what's going on. I have a brilliant drug that can save people's lives. I've been working on it for years and I can't get it out of the gate. What am I doing wrong?" Deepak replied with a stunning answer: "You're trying too hard!" She had never heard of such a thing. Her whole life had been about the opposite, about striving, about doing enough no matter what the obstacle. This foreign concept opened a new door to her thinking.

Deepak invited her to his retreat center in Lancaster, Massachusetts, where she learned meditation, experienced massage, and came down from the intensity of drug trials. When she left, her experience gave her the impetus to begin making lifestyle changes as well. She improved her diet, started exercising, meditated daily, and saw homeopathic doctors. This new lifestyle changed her perspective on "trying too hard" and she began to feel more relaxed about everything, including drug trials. Later that year, a potential pharaceutical investor heard her speak and was impressed by her manner and her interest in Peptide T. They met afterward and he asked her what the funding status of the drug was. She was so embarrassed about how things were that she lied and told him, "We've got a great possibility coming up with a Japanese company that's about to come on line." The truth was that the Japanese company was a far bet and she needed an investor that could come up with millions to bring the drug to the market, or the drug might be permanently in danger. When they finished their conversation, he said, "Well, give me a call if you need anything." About a month later, as she was facing bankruptcy and the loss of the drug, the phone rang. It was the potential investor, calling to check on the status of the drug. He asked if her Japanese investor had been confirmed. She told him no. The Japanese company

Good Business

MR. CHUNG HAD provided goods to a large oil company in the Far East. When the prices rose, he billed his client, Mr. Wu, accordingly. But Mr. Wu continued to pay the old rates.

Mr. Chung visited Mr. Wu five times. Each time his client refused to make up the increases. At their last meeting Mr. Chung said, "I'd like to sever this relationship. I no longer want to do business with you. We cannot keep our business relationship alive."

The client became insulted and started yelling. He demanded the name of Mr. Chung's manager, and he demanded to speak to the president. Mr. Chung gave him all the information he asked for. As the businessman was about to leave, Mr. Wu said, "Wait a minute. I don't like doing business like this. Let's talk about it." They sat down again, agreed to the new pricing, and have worked together ever since.

Sometimes you must let go before you can get what you want. Mr. Chung let go twice. First, he was willing to let this account close. Keeping a client who didn't pay his bills was a bad business practice anyway. But rather than fight, he was ready to cut his losses and move on.

Then he let go of his anger and pride, and returned to the negotiations. It might have been easier to storm out of the office, let the client go over his head, and let someone else handle the account. But he put his ego aside, and was able to resume his dialogue in a more cooperative tone.

had fallen through. His next question was, "How much do you need?" She was back in business. He supplied her the necessary millions and the testing began. Deepak's advice had come full swing. By letting go of trying too hard, she had gotten everything that she needed.

A Striking Lesson

Twice today, on two different talk shows, I listened to the stories of people who had been wrongfully imprisoned, found guilty of crimes they did not commit. The first was a mother of two teenagers who had been accused of killing her husband. The second was an African American man accused of rape.

In both cases, nearly ten years passed before evidence surfaced exonerating the prisoners. They were freed, but there was no way to reclaim the time that had been taken from them.

What struck me most was the attitude they had in common. Neither was bitter, angry, or vengeful. They both put it the same way: "I've already lost so much. Why would I waste my freedom? I'd be giving up more than I've already lost, but this time, it would be my own choosing."

Imagine how you'd feel if you'd survived the ultimate injustice. A mother unable to witness the milestones of her children's lives; a man stripped of his dignity and robbed of his self-determination. They both recognize that anger would do more damage to themselves, and would still fail to right the wrong they'd endured.

These two people have truly risen above it all. Could you be so noble, even under less extreme circumstances? In *The Way of the Wizard*, Deepak Chopra reminds us: "Because we all want things, it's easy to fall into the trap of constantly working, worrying, and struggling to get what we want. Yet, if you let go, the mechanics of desire take care of themselves."

Are you ready to learn the formula for real change? Are you willing to try new ways of speaking, thinking, and acting for new results? Get ready. The dance is about to begin.

SIX

The Solution to Your Problems: Awareness

Our goal is peace now—this very instant. It is central to our happiness that our years, long or short, be free of anger and that your body can be used as a means of giving others the gift of kindness.

—*Gerald G. Jampolsky, M.D.*, Teach Only Love

Shall We Dance?

Awareness exists at different levels. Am I aware of myself and what I'm doing? Am I aware of you and what you're doing? People assume they're more aware of themselves than they are of others, but the opposite is true. We tend to take more notice of what other people do, and examine them more carefully.

Awareness is more circular, flowing outward, inward, and back again. Notice the relationship between cause and effect. How does what you say affect me? How does my response affect you? Conversation is a dance. If you fail to notice that your partner has stopped waltzing and has started to cha-cha, you're going to get stepped on.

When I go into a class about difficult people, the first thing I ask is, "What is your difficult person doing?" Immediately I get a response: "They do this or that to me." And then I ask, "How are you when you're with them? What are you like?" Most of the time people hesitate. They don't know or they don't remember. If they remember anything at all, it's their emotions. They don't know what their body is doing, what their words were, or how they were spoken.

During a seminar, Eleanor was describing a fight she'd had with a difficult neighbor. All she remembers is that as she talked, her anger escalated and spun her into an altered emotional state. "I didn't even know what I was saying," she recalls. "It was like my brain was disconnected from what was coming out of my mouth." Some people describe this feeling as blind rage.

Nor does she remember what her body was doing: whether her teeth or fists were clenched, whether her torso was tilted forward, whether her face was flushed. She is certain of one thing: She was furious. The fury was in control, and Eleanor was out of control.

Defining Emotions

Researchers have discovered physiological evidence for emotional outbursts. There's a whole separate circuitry in the body that acts independently of the rational brain, which perpetuates the habit of anger. By understanding this response you can learn to interrupt it, or at least to accept it as a natural biological process.

Daniel Goleman, Ph.D., in his book *Emotional Intelligence,* examines this phenomenon. He explains that the *amygdala,* a pair of almond-shaped structures in the brain discovered by Joseph LeDoux, are responsible for these intense and immediate emotional responses. In this primordial part of the brain, stimuli fire emergency messages and short-circuit the brain's reasoning pathways. The amygdala scan incoming information and release stress-related biochemicals into the bloodstream. They're triggered by fast-acting stimuli, causing what Goleman refers to as an "amygdala hijack." The fight-or-flight response kicks in, leading to impulsive reactions from our emotional center before logic even has a chance to analyze them.

Amygdala responses can also build slowly over time, gathering strength like a storm. These signals come from the neocortex, after it has had the chance to carefully consider some past slight or injustice. In either case, the amygdala release can cause a wide range of sensations from mild irritation to blind fury.

According to Goleman, during a rage the body is

flooded; the heart beats up to thirty times more per minute, the muscles clench, and breathing is impaired. The body steeps in anger, infecting and affecting all systems, dampening reason and control.

The amygdala are also the archives of emotional memory, warehousing our most intense experiences. They examine new events and compare them to the spectrum of past responses. A friend fails to meet you for lunch, and you're furious. But you aren't reacting only to the hurt of someone standing you up, but the hurt of every time you've ever been let down. This explains why when difficult people upset us, it isn't just a momentary upset, but a cumulative one, often eliciting that all-too-familiar volcanic eruption. We aren't just upset now. We are upset for now and for every other moment that led up to it.

Adding Up to Change

The way to get from awareness to knowledge is through inquiry. Knowing what motivates people can help you understand behavior, and understanding gives you the opportunity to change it.

Awareness + Knowledge + Action = Change

If you can plug in the factors of this equation, you will alter your situation. Let's look at each element.

Step 1: Awareness

Are you clear about what it is your difficult person does to upset you? Be aware of the specific behavior you don't like. Don't apply subjective labels, but rather identify the action that sets you off.

The Subjective Label (Assessment)	What's Really Happening
He's a jerk.	*He rejects my ideas.*
She's rude.	*She never says good morning, please, or thank you. She dismisses my suggestions.*
He is moody.	*In the morning he is happy, but by lunch, he's snapping at everyone. You don't know what to expect.*
She is abusive.	*She screams, curses, and insults me.*

| He's intimidating. | *He stares at me, crosses his arms, and then insists things be done his way. He claims to be the only one who knows how to do things.* |
| She's a liar. | *She promised me a raise, but so far my pay has stayed the same.* |

By defining the behavior, you add a level of objectivity, and can view the person as a human being. We can relate to human beings more easily when we separate them and their value from their actions.

Step 2: Knowledge

Use the insight you gain from this book to understand why difficult people behave the way they do. Pick one new technique a week to try and see what result comes from that. For instance, you might pick a BOP option this week to try, and see what results you get. Next week you might examine the labels in Step 1 in order to try new thinking. You can get a "solution buddy" to help you implement these ideas and report to that person weekly to see how these ideas are working. Contemplate and discuss what ideas are coming forward. Mentally release available options. Be ready to change your behavior.

Step 3: Action

Now that you understand how your actions and re-actions can be altered, you can note in your journal what's working and what isn't. Reward the behavior you want to see repeated. Do more of what works. Drop what doesn't. Compare notes with your "solution buddy" and keep moving. Note what it is that you have to let go of in order to move forward.

Step 4: Change

Enjoy it! Notice how your thinking changes as a result of new behaviors. What impact is this having not so much on the other person, but on your attitude and relationship toward them?

Who's in the Middle?

Is your difficult person not giving you enough attention? Does he ignore your questions, buzz away from conversations, answer phone calls even though you are in midsentence? Are you being expected to carry your end of the relationship with too little information from him? It's possible that he is trying to look, act, and feel important.

During a mentoring session, I complained to my mentor that I couldn't slow down, and that I was always running behind. My mentor asked if being late and rushing around made me feel important. I realized then that it does. He explained the only reason a person would pursue that aura of importance is because he or she doesn't feel important.

What does being important get me? When I was a child, my mother used to stand me in the center of a room crowded with relatives, who would clap for me. I felt bathed in love and admiration. Calling attention to myself by being overbooked and showing up late was like saying, "Look at me, I am very important."

Awareness of this part of me was the first step toward changing it. I started letting go of my need to appear important to others. I am important to me, and being important to anyone else is irrelevant. This may or may not change what I'm doing immediately, but it changes the essence of why I do it, and takes off a lot of the pressure. Ultimately, it will lead to changes in what I do. I couldn't change my behavior until I looked closely at what I was doing and why. Increasing your awareness, knowledge and action are key to unlocking your patterns with difficult people. Even if you've done all these things, how do you navigate around the dysfunctional people you encounter? It's time to learn a few maneuvering techniques. Now that we know about us, what about *them*?

Thought into Action

MAKE THE DELIBERATE decision to counteract those instantaneous amygdala responses. Don't react to the emotional moment. Do nothing for ten seconds. The next time someone does something that sets you off, wait. Allow the release of anger and hormones to wash through your system before you respond.

Now it's time to be your own coach. Use reason and logic to reverse the anger. Tell yourself to stop, deliberately analyze the situation, and ask yourself some questions. Does this person really mean to make me angry? Is my response appropriate to the situation? Can I examine what he or she has done with a measure of compassion? Have I ever done something like this to someone else?

Take a time-out. Count to ten. Recognize the amygdala's ability to take over and lead you to rash actions. Take your thinking back into the arena of logic. In time this will become your automatic response.

PART TWO

Personality Types and Patterns of Behavior

Psychological courage entails a cleansing of the doors of perception, allowing us to see things as they really are rather than through the distorted lens of the past. The more we are cleansed of expectations, the more we see what is and the more we can respond to it creatively.

—Joan Borysenko, Ph.D., Fire in the Soul

SEVEN

Snakes, Apes, Bees, and Other Animals in Your Kingdom

Name the Animal

When you think of a difficult person, do you get a picture of an evil ogre with red, beady eyes, a hook nose, and a hairy mole? If you've already encountered a fair number of difficult people (and most adults have), you know that difficult people come in many different sizes, shapes, and colors. Few visual clues will alert you to difficult people before you engage them. But there are some signs you can read if you're aware of them.

Suppose you need to change an airline ticket. As you approach the reservation agent's window, you observe the following signs: Her hand is gripping the telephone so tightly her knuckles are white; her shoulders are taut; her brow is furrowed. When she looks up at you, her eyes narrow, and her lips tighten.

Frank and Ernest

THE SHARP POINT ON THE SPEAR
SHOWS YOUR AGGRESSIVENESS,
THE SHORT HORNS ON THE
BUFFALO INDICATE THAT
YOU'RE BASICALLY
INSECURE, WHILE
THE MAN AND
THE DUCK.....

© 1997 Thaves/Reprinted with permission. Newspaper dist by NEA, Inc.

By reading these nonverbal signals, you give yourself an advantage. You know that you're about to have a close encounter with a difficult person. You can benefit from a few seconds of mental preparation, and you can call up some of the coping skills gleaned from these pages.

More often, the difficulty you will run up against with an individual will not be so obvious, and may in fact change depending on the situation. There are nine distinct types of difficult personalities. Understanding the different types and why they act the way they do can be a great help when plotting your relationship strategy.

The Nine Types of Difficult Personalities

Difficult personalities generally fall under two major categories: aggressive and passive. Aggressive people are loud; their gestures are intimidating; they try to plow through others with force. They interrupt, push, and manipulate. They're argumentative and they project a hateful attitude.

Aggressive people can be either situationally difficult or genetically difficult. The former can't negotiate life's bumps and curves; the latter take pleasure in being difficult. Let's look at the different aggressive personalities in detail. Chances are you'll recognize at least one.

The Hostile Apes

They're loud, explosive, and rude. Not only don't they consider your needs, but they don't stop to think you might have any. Responding to an ape in a similar apelike way is a waste of time.

To get along with an ape, be assertive, not aggressive. Look him in the eye so he knows you mean business. Your confidence and strength will diminish his. And don't be passive either. Force or submission on your part only plays into his game. If he interrupts you, say, "Hang on, let me finish," or simply hold up your hand.

If you say, "No way am I doing that!" you're being aggressive. But if you say, "Let's discuss our options," you're being assertive. The difference can have a big impact on the way your exchange goes.

There's no point in reasoning with people who are unreasonable. They aren't interested in issues; they're too involved in the game. Take yourself out of the game. Your body may be there, but your emotions are elsewhere. Here's a six-step approach to dealing with aggressive people and the stress reactions they cause.

Step 1: Neutralize

First, neutralize by breathing. Fill your abdomen with air, pushing it out like a balloon. Then release. Fill and release. Keep your hand on your abdomen while you are doing this, and watch as it is pushed out and in. Breathing releases your stress and helps neutralize on a physical level.

Then change the thought. Your mind is working against you. But it can work to support you. When your difficult person approaches, your mind starts playing tapes. "Oh gosh, here she comes! I can't handle this today. I don't have the patience for this." Your frustration level, your blood pressure, and your upset are already elevated, and she hasn't even come through the door. Then your mind waits for her to do those things that bother you so much, and when she does, they trigger your patterned responses. You can't progress in the relationship, because your reactions have become so automatic.

In *The Healer Within,* Roger Jahnke offers us advice on how to strengthen our minds: "Our choice of attitudes and mental influences maximize the activity of our naturally occurring self-healing capability. When we choose to think, believe, and act from a position of power, refusing to be a victim of circumstances, the healer within is automatically strengthened. When we refuse to live under the influence of worry and doubt, the internal medicine is enriched."

Next time you hear your difficult person coming, try a new thought. "I'm ready for you. I can do this. I can handle this. You're my teacher. I'm going to handle this better. I'm going to become a better person." Pick one thought and repeat it. Boost your strength, and relax.

In their book *Executive EQ*, Robert K. Cooper and Ayman Sawaf outline a process called entrainment, "discovered in 1665 by Dutch scientist Christian Huygens, by which rhythms of voice and emotion are drawn into productive balance with each other."

They suggest that you "join a dialogue by talking slowly and calmly, not denying any of the emotions present, but not getting battered about by them either. As a meeting or discussion heats up, change the rhythm by speaking calmly and more slowly, which draws everyone into great awareness of the dialogue process and can begin to open minds and hearts."

When an affront sparks your hormonal engine, continuing to drive the engine increases the flood of adrenaline and emotion. Next time, allow the hormone surge to wash through your body. For a moment, don't react or act. The sensation will wane, and rational thought will return. It's OK to be quiet for a moment. Sometimes showing command of language is saying nothing at all.

Step 2: Change the Body

The thought tapes playing in your head show on your face and in your body. You can pretend to be calm and open to this person, but your underlying stress will betray you. When you hold a thought in your mind, it's reflected in your face. Your mouth is saying, "Hi, John! How's it going?" but your mind is whispering, "Go away!"

What John sees is the mixed messages, and whether he is conscious of it or not, he reads your dislike. Does he respond to what you say? Or to the signals you're sending? If he perceives that you're shaken up, he'll try to shake you up more.

But if the thought in your head changes, and you can square your shoulders, look him in the eye, and really be in control, he'll sense that too. Then he'll wonder, "Why isn't she losing it today?" He'll be caught off guard, and his efforts will be derailed.

You can also use body language to aid communication. Lean toward him slightly. Put your hand on your chin. Point toward your brain. Slight alterations in your posture show that you're interested in what he has to say.

Intention creates outcome. Changing your thought creates the potential for a different outcome. What is your intention?

Step 3: Listen

Now you've neutralized, collected yourself, arranged your posture, and prepared yourself. To do what? Listen.

You must listen. Not just with open ears, but with an open mind. Be in the conversation 100 percent. If she doesn't feel like she's got your attention, she'll find a way to get it. And you won't like it. She'll be rude, she'll be demanding. She'll become more aggressive. Or she'll walk away.

👉 **EXAMPLES OF SELF-NEUTRALIZATION:**

- "This isn't personal. It's not about me."
- "I'm in control of me. I can handle this."
- Imagine yourself protected in a castle.
- Change your posture by putting your hand on your belly button and focusing your head up. This accesses the core of your body and will give you more power.

👉 **SAMPLE STATEMENTS/QUESTIONS FOR ACKNOWLEDGING, SAVING FACE, VALIDATING, AND LISTENING:**

- "You may be right; what you're saying is possible."
- "Can I ask you something?"
- "I'm sorry you feel that way; it wasn't my intention to hurt you."
- "Tell me what I said/did to make you feel that way."
- "Let's talk about that."
- "I'm confused. I don't understand why this is upsetting you."
- "I didn't know you were feeling so strongly about this. Can you make it more clear for me?"

Step 4: Shift Hemispheres

If you listen, you begin to diffuse the situation. Then you can move the conversation forward. A person who is talking emotionally, irrationally, and illogically is operating with the right hemisphere of the brain. By asking questions and forcing him to think logically, you turn on his left hemisphere—the logical, problem-solving area. Use words like *specifically*, *technically*, *exactly*. Getting the person to be specific and to examine the problem logically fires neurons in the left hemisphere, and lowers the volume coming from the emotional center.

If Jake says, "You're stupid, you're an idiot, you screwed everything up!" it's an emotional response. You can say, "You're a moron!" but you'd only be stimulating the emotions further. Now you're both juiced on emotion. But if you say, "Okay, let's have some information. Specifically, what did I do to make you feel this way? Give me the details," he is forced into halting the tirade, switching to the practical side of his brain, and gathering your answer from his data bank. He may jump back to the emotional, but you can keep pulling him back to the problem solving side by asking those "-ly" questions. Daniel Goleman refers to this as "distracting the mind."

When you've given Jake a chance to vent, you can focus him on some productive dialogue. "I can see you're angry and you needed to let me know about it. Now it's time for us to talk things over."

Think of an angry outburst as a lit match. It will flare and burn, but only for a few seconds. Your best defense is to let the match burn itself out. Don't argue. Don't agree. Just hang with it. Without fuel, it will extinguish itself. If this doesn't work, check the section in this chapter titled "The Complaining Lizards."

Step 5: Find a Solution

Now that you have the person's attention and have switched gears you can suggest a solution. Consider a counteroffer. This is the negotiation process. Discuss the implications of both. How does your way affect me? How does mine affect you? Are there other options we haven't considered yet?

Devote 20 percent of the time to the problem, and 80 percent to the solution. Then you can move on to step 6.

👆 **SAMPLE STATEMENTS/QUESTIONS FOR MOVING TOWARD A SOLUTION:**

- "There are a lot of important things to talk about. Let's figure them out and do them one at a time."
- "Where do you suggest we start?"
- "How can I help? What can I do?"

Step 6: Action Agreement

Now that you've discussed solutions you can propose a course of action. Whatever it is, it should get you out of complaint mode. "How about if we review this and talk again tomorrow?" "Let's do some research and find out more." "Call Fred and get his insight."

Find some common ground. If you can't come up with a solution on your own, ask him to help. "What would you like to see happen?" "What would be acceptable?"

Sometimes he'll get stuck, and you'll have to help him accept reality. He may say, "We can't perform with this little money. We need a new budget." Your response? "There isn't any possibility of that happening. Now, what can we do to work with what we've got?" Team up to explore solutions. Get on the same page, use the same language, and examine your options—together.

Next, make a contract. You agree to do something. He agrees to do something. And you both agree what the next step will be. "Let's both review our department's financial situation and see where we can find some extra money. Then we can meet again on Wednesday and talk more about it." The agreement may be as simple as letting it go for a while and revisiting it at another time.

A few years ago I had the opportunity to practice these six steps. I was on my way to a lecture by Bob Thurman, an author who just finished a book called *Inner Revolution*. (He was the first American monk ordained by the Dalai Lama.) My thinking was to leave my car in the parking lot across from the metro, stop in to see him, and then swing back and have dinner in one of my favorite restaurants, which was located in the shopping center next to the parking lot. I got there a little before 5 P.M. and then rushed downtown for the lecture. I had felt a little anxious running around all day, and when I arrived the hurriedness of the day was still around me. When Bob began to speak, that changed. He talked about the third noble truth in Buddhism, which says there is an end to suffering: "All beings can attain that end to suffering." He said, "We get angry because we think our lives are the center of the universe. When we come into conflict with the universe we want the universe to fit our mold and it doesn't. We cannot fight the universe and our thinking that we are different from it." He went on to say that we have to take responsibility for what we think and say. "Our thoughts are evolutionary actions," he proclaimed. He urged us to take more responsibility for the "vibes" we send out, and how we affect those around us and those not around us. It's kind of like putting a rock in a pond and watching the ripple effect. We are more connected than we know.

As I sat and listened to his words, a sense of calmness overtook me. By the time I left, my earlier state of anxious rushing was replaced by a centered and easygoing lightness. I was relaxed and hungry. It was now almost 8 P.M. As I got off the metro and crossed the street to the parking lot, I noticed something was different. Something was missing. Within seconds I realized what it was. My car! Still remaining in that state and just saying to myself, "Oh, that's interesting. My car is gone," I entered the restaurant, where I happen to know the owner, and told him the news. Not only was I the second of his customers to be towed, but it had happened to him as well, and his lawyer was pursuing the matter. "OK. Great, but how do I get my car back," I wondered out loud. He quickly went to get the number of the towing place and I called, only to be greeted by a Neanderthal on the other end. The second I mentioned that I had parked my car in the lot to have dinner there, he began his diatribe: "Your car has been in that lot over two hours," he yelled, at a decibel level high enough for a rock concert. "There is a sign. Didn't you see the sign. YOU ARE IN VIOLATION!" Well, so much for my centered state. I lost it for a moment and accepted his invitation to banter. "I went out and came back here to have dinner," I screamed. "So what if it took more than two hours!" He then returned to his monologue. At that point my awareness kicked in. I realized this guy was the poster child for jerks and that I wasn't going to get anywhere with him. Thank God for the six steps. I had already neutralized, so I moved into step 3: listening. I sat and waited, not giving him any fuel for the fire. Within seconds we had skipped step 4 and he had moved into step 5 (solution) without my saying another word. "Do you want your car back?" he asked in a more reserved tone. "Here are the directions. You need ninety bucks in cash and a driver's license." Step 6 was in full gear. I didn't exactly agree with the terms of getting my car back, but if I wanted it, I didn't have a choice. George, the owner of the restaurant, was kind enough to drive me to the towing site a few miles away. On the way over, I decided not to engage with this barbarian. I imagined myself with a protective shield, a force field around me that protected me, one that he couldn't enter. I felt contained in that and strong when we approached the door. I got out and, without looking at the guy, handed him a $100 bill. He told me he didn't have change, so George told me to wait while he went back to the store.

He left and I went over to the side of the building away from "that guy" to wait. I felt no need to be nice or make conversation. I didn't care if he liked me; I really didn't care what he thought about me. As I stood there and waited I heard a rustling noise—and a ten-week-old puppy stumbled through the door. I fell in love. I let down my guard, bent over, and started talking to the dog in high-pitched doggie talk. "Hi sweetie, yes aren't you a cute thing," I squealed. I melted.

When the jerk saw this side of me he wanted to engage. "You love dogs, don't you?" he wondered out loud. I didn't acknowledge him. I continued playing with the dog. It felt so good to not have to please someone. I was pleasing myself and in that moment it was enough. Soon George came back with the money, we paid, and I said good-bye to the dog. I could feel the jerk watching me, hoping I would change my mind and talk to him. I didn't want anything to do with his negative volatile energy. I kept my container around me when I felt him addressing me. As I drove off, I felt him watching and I stared straight ahead.

Later, I discussed this incident with anthropologist Dr. Kanu Kogod. I wondered out loud why the man had continued to speak to me when I so blatantly ignored him. She said, "Being shunned means you die. Shunning is a way to control people. It came from our primordial need to survive when we existed as hunters and gatherers and needed to live and cooperate in community. Language was necessary. You can't kill a buffalo by yourself. You can't even carry firewood without assistance. We have always needed each other in order to function. It was an old re-active pattern. It's in our DNA."

I took a few lessons from that incident. First, I learned that when I recognize and focus on my own state, it's easy to avoid taking on someone else's. When I lost it with "that man" on the phone in the restaurant, I experienced what it felt like to give my power away, and I didn't want to do that again. Being focused on my state instead of his allowed me to feel solid and confident in myself. Second, I learned that I don't need others' approval and acceptance to feel OK about myself. Yes, some people's assessments and opinions about me or what I do are important to me. But I learned that it doesn't hold true for everyone. I don't have to "make nice" when I really don't want to. It allows me to be real. Last, I learned not to park my car in that lot more than two hours. Reward the behavior you want to see repeated. No reward there.

> *Our goal is peace now—this very instant. It is*
> *central to our happiness that our years, long or*
> *short, be free of anger and that your body be used as*
> *a means of giving others the gift of kindness.*
>
> —*Gerald G. Jampolsky, M.D.,* Teach Only Love

The Rambling Hyenas

Hyenas aren't truly aggressive; they're just plain annoy-ing. They make lots of noise, but rarely say anything valuable. Hyenas use a flood of words to get attention, but the tactic usually works against them. Instead of listening, you tune them out and wait for them to run out of steam.

You answer the phone, and it's your friendly neighborhood hyena. You could put down the phone, take a shower, fix a cup of coffee, come back to the phone, and she's still talking. She probably didn't even know you were gone.

Is she giving you too much information? Is she telling you something you aren't interested in? How can you get her to the point?

To get along with a hyena, remember that sticking with her diatribes is permission to continue. If you shake your head and say "uh-huh," the rambler thinks you want to hear what she is saying. She thinks you want to know, and if you give any signals to support that theory, she'll take it as a license to keep going.

Don't take the offensive, either. Telling a hyena she's rambling or to hurry up and get to the point isn't effective; it isn't even nice. Bring it back to yourself by saying, "I'm not with you right now. What specifically do I need to know?" or, "You've lost me. What is it you're trying to say?" Direct and redirect the conversation. Point her in the direction you feel it needs to go. Ask, "What do you want me to know?"

The Sarcastic Bees

A bee stings. Usually it gets him a laugh, or a little attention. Sometimes he uses it as a way to separate someone from the group, making someone who is weak or vulnerable the butt of his jokes and a target of derision.

He might make comments like, "You're on time today," when you get to a meeting late. Or "Nice job" when you've made a mistake. His sarcasm often escalates when other people are around; that's when he entertains the hive.

Sarcasm is the only way he can relate to you. Your job is to let him know, directly or indirectly, "This is not how I want you to address me."

When aggressive people get upset, this is how they act. They fall into patterned responses, and don't think they have any other choices. We have to look at ways of barring their effect on us. We have to find a way of relating to them that changes their reactions to us, not because we are manipulating them, or because we are hoping they will change, but because we want to feel better about ourselves. We must give ourselves dignity and respect, and not expect them to provide that for us. We have to give less attention to how they react, and to our desire to make them react differently.

Let go of your concern for their reactions. Letting go detaches us from our emotional entanglements and gives less importance to the way difficult people treat us.

To get along with a bee, foremost, don't encourage his

behavior. Don't laugh when he's trying to be funny, and don't join in when he's doing it to someone else.

Or you can bring it to his attention. Get him alone and say calmly, "That really hurt my feelings. It felt like you were cutting me down. Did you mean it that way?" If he knows he's hurt you, he'll probably feel guilty. He needs to know that his jabs are causing harm. If he responds by saying you are too sensitive, you can counteract that by saying "I might be, but I thought you would want to know how your words affect other people." With this response, you don't demand change, you invite it. You leave him with the consequences of his own behavior and his own choice for change.

Recently I spoke in an organization that housed a lot of bees. In one of the seminars someone cited an example of how a person on her team repeatedly makes uncomfortable sexual remarks, racial slurs, and ethnic jabs. "How do the other people on the team handle this," I asked. She responded, "We all laugh uncomfortably, hoping he'll stop." "Does he?" I inquired. "No," she said. "He's been doing it for five years." This bee has been rewarded for his stings for five years and no one had bothered to say anything to him or treat him differently. After class we talked about the possibility of someone either speaking to him or as a team agreeing not to laugh, to in fact be silent, when he makes offending comments. She agreed to try the silent approach first. After two team meetings of no response, his offensiveness stopped.

The Know-It-All Owls

Know anyone with the "my way or the highway" mentality? These are the know-it-all owls. They know everything about everything. They refuse to listen to your opinions, or to even consider that another opinion besides their own even exists.

Owls are making up for insecurity. They pretend to know everything, when in fact they feel like they know nothing. An owl relies on external approval to feel validated. But like a leaky bucket, the moments of being right never really add up to fullness. Sometimes they take on more responsibility than others in an organization so they can not only look right, but be visible in the process.

When challenging an owl, you're touching that part of her that feels so inadequate, the part she is working so diligently to cover up. She can't be right without making you wrong. It's as if you are a float in a pool; when she pushes you down, she floats up.

To get along with an owl, instead of saying "I disagree with you," give her the illusion that she's right and you like her idea. Give her the validation she craves. Then introduce your own idea. Don't negate hers, but rather add yours. "That's a great perspective; I never thought of that. Here's what I thought . . ." or "That's good. And how about this?" Get rid of the word *but* when speaking to an owl; it makes her think you're brushing her opinions aside.

Don't discount an owl's opinion. Allow the possibility to exist that she's right.

When Feedback Works with an Owl

Harry was the kind of guy you didn't want at meetings. He was argumentative, arrogant, opinionated, and stubborn. His superiors often accused him of jamming his viewpoints down other people's throats. What most people never seemed to understand about Harry was that he was much more confident than he was arrogant. On several occasions, he would question his seniors in public about something they said or implied. To most present, it appeared as if Harry was criticizing these individuals. In fact, Harry was simply trying to get the facts straight. Harry always wanted to get to the heart of the matter and was not sensitive to others' feelings when he was doing it. It wasn't that he didn't care how they felt; he just felt that the truth was much more important. His truth.

One day a supervisor said, "You're the only one who knows how to get these programs working. But because of how you treat people, no one wants you around. If you could take a different approach, be less aggressive, then people would do it your way."

He thought about it and realized he'd been his own worst enemy. It was time to change. Harry had been in a constant state of frustration. He was brighter and more experienced than most of his peers, yet he wasn't getting anywhere professionally. He had in fact been passed over for promotion, which had almost never happened to someone with his talents. He thought about his situation over the years, and concluded that he had been doing himself in. In every case he could think of, he had in fact been "right." What good had it done him? He was not getting the promotions or opportunities that others with less intelligence or competence were getting.

What was he doing wrong? His arrogance and attitude were doing him in. What good is knowing what needs to be done, if you can't present it in the proper way? What if you could actually make it appear that it was someone else's idea? His ego was too big to allow something like that to happen. He had to be considered the one who had the idea. He had to be considered the brilliant one. He was doomed by his own needy ego. Such a sad situation. So much talent gone to waste. Unfortunately, at this time in his life, Harry knew he had a problem, knew something had to be done about it, but didn't really know how to change the situation. After a week of internal evaluation he decided to do something different.

At his next meeting, he behaved much differently. For the first time ever, he gave people options instead of dictating solutions. First he said, "Here's how we're doing it, which doesn't seem to be working. Here's how we've done it in the past, which I liked, but you didn't. The third method combines both." He let others feel that they had some control. He humbled himself, gave his co-workers the information, and let them make the decisions based on his recommendations. But he did not dictate.

After the meeting his boss touched him on the shoulder and congratulated him. By modifying his approach, he had achieved his goal without alienating everyone and tarnishing his own reputation. Harry has continued to apply this way of being and it has now become a part of his nature. As a result he is experiencing more success and personal satisfaction.

You can't give feedback until you know what it is. Awareness is critical. At the same time, the person receiving the feedback has to have an openness to what you have to offer. The more open you are, the more open they will likely be, increasing the probability of change.

The Complaining Lizards

Lizards love to complain. It's fun for them. But they need an audience. To them, the cup is always half empty and it's usually dirty too. Whatever you say, they find fault. They revel in the problem. The last thing they're interested in is a solution.

Lizards are especially unhealthy in the workplace. Either they hang in the background, infecting morale, or they force others to waste time dealing with their gripes. They poison the atmosphere. Everyone is happier at work when problems with difficult co-workers are addressed.

To get along with a lizard, get her away from problems and into solutions. Since she isn't interested in solutions, you're not going to change the way she thinks. What you will change, though, is where she seeks attention. Make it clear that you aren't going to feed her hunger. Don't nod your head, apologize, agree, or sympathize. She'll go look for someone else who will.

How to stop complainers? Use directed questions. "What would you like to see happen here?" "What do you see yourself doing to settle this issue?" "How can I help you handle this right now?" If her complaining continues, set limits. "I've got a meeting. Why don't you go think about this and then let me know where you want to go with it." Always bring it back to her, and how she can arrive at a resolution. Let her know that when she is with you, you won't allow her complaining behavior to thrive.

Now let's look at the passive behaviors. Their motivations are similar, but produce different kinds of behavior. On the outside, they seem agreeable, but their compliance comes at a price. They're angry without taking responsibility for it. Passives lie, pretend to agree, cheat, and offer backhanded compliments. They might comply maliciously. For instance, they'll let a mistake you made go uncorrected so you look bad. The idea with the passives is to elicit response. Ask questions that encourage elaboration. Try following conversations with passives with an open-ended question like, "What is your perception or assessment of what we just talked about?" Getting them to talk, and helping them feel accepted for what they have to say, will encourage trust and true dialogue with them in the future.

The Unresponsive Snails

Snails lurk in the corners, hang in the shadows, and call as little attention to themselves as they can. They are unresponsive, and when you do get answers, they divulge very little information. "How's the workload?" you ask. "Fine," they whisper.

To get along with a snail, remember that snails are very reserved and quiet in their manner. Build a rapport, gain his trust, and you'll have more success with this type. Align your tone with his. If you tend to be bold, speak softly. If you tend to gesture a lot, fold your hands in your lap. Then mimic his body posture. If he leans back, lean back. If he leans forward, do the same. He'll start to think of you as more like him, more understanding of his nature.

Ask open-ended questions, ones that can't be answered with a simple yes or no. "Can you give me some information about the project you're working on?" is better than "Is your project going well?"

A snail processes more slowly. Give him time to think about his answers. "I've got a meeting with the client on Monday. Can you give me an update on your project by Friday afternoon?"

The Overcommitting, Underdelivering Snakes

Like other passives, snakes seek approval, and will do anything to earn it—even if it means making commitments they can't live up to. They wiggle into your heart by promising you the world. Then they disappoint you because they're overextended or become distracted by something else.

To get along with a snake, you must learn to recognize snakelike behavior so that you can exercise some options. If you know that a person is legendary for breaking promises, you can ride her along the way. She says she'll have a report on your desk Friday? Call Monday, Tuesday, Wednesday. Keep reminding her. Make sure she knows how high a priority this is for you.

The other option poses some risk for you, and may make you look bad for a bit, but it will surely cure your snake. People are motivated by reward; we move toward pleasure and away from pain. The way to inflict pain on a snake is to let her fail. Let her feel the full weight of consequences that result from her inaction. Don't take up the slack; make her bear the responsibility she sought in the first place.

Tim Flynn, the founder and former president of U.S. Office Products (which owns Mail Boxes, Etc.), told me of a scenario where he had to work on a project with someone who constantly gave information and suggestions and had an immense need to be right. He called the person a nuisance. Because the person had a high need not only to be right, but also to be involved in every aspect of a project, Tim continued to give him more responsibility and overload him with information and responsibility. It ultimately overwhelmed him. This person ended up not being able to complete his responsibility and, out of guilt, he took himself off the project. Fortunately, it was arranged so that his responsibility wasn't crucial to the success of the project.

The Dumbfounded Donkeys

Donkeys will stand rooted in one place unless they're forcibly led away. They aren't go-getters. They don't initiate. They have trouble making decisions. They expect you to make the decisions, to take direction, to take the risks. Then they can blame you when things go awry.

Why? Like most other dysfunctional personalities, donkeys are afraid. They fear they will make the wrong choice. They'll fail. They'll look bad. It's safer to do nothing than to do the wrong thing.

To get along with a donkey, give him a set of choices. Point out the likely outcomes, good and bad, for each option. Offer your opinion, guiding him toward the path you'd like to see him pick. Explain your reasons.

Then take some of the pressure off. Show that the repercussions of a mistake won't end the world. Yes, it's possible to misstep. But mistakes alter your life, give you clarity of vision, add up as experience, and lead to wisdom.

And when a donkey makes a tough decision that leads to a positive outcome, recognize his achievement. Let others know what an accomplishment this was for him. Reward him for sticking out his neck.

The Prickly Porcupines

Don't turn your back on a porcupine—you're likely to get stabbed! These are the classic backstabbers. They sabotage, speak negatively about you in others' presence, and often say one thing and do another. Their outward smiles are cover for their inner fire and vengeance.

To get along with a porcupine, you must understand what motivates her so that you can limit the effects she has on your life. She's resentful. She's insecure. She's not getting ahead. The only way she sees to move forward is to move somebody else back.

You can do one of two things: Ignore her and let other people make their own assessments about you, or approach her directly. Use a calm, gentle tone, and avoid accusations that would make her defensive: "Listen, I know you said this thing to this person. I'm aware of it and I'm uncomfortable with it. I'd rather you tell me if you've got concerns or issues instead of talking about it with someone else."

She may deny it. But you've let her know that she's not getting away with it, and what she's saying is getting back to you. If she has any conscience at all, she'll feel guilty and ashamed that she's been caught. A backstabber's satisfaction comes in part from thinking she's been clever, sneaky, and underhanded. Take that away, and it becomes a less enjoyable deceit.

Another option is to move around the person as if she

and her claims don't exist. Don't focus on them at all. That's what Luther did with Connie when he started at the news station with her. Luther and Connie co-hosted a radio show. Connie was the veteran, and she resented the success and attention that newcomer Luther was garnering.

Whenever she had the chance, she would talk about Luther behind his back. If she couldn't think of anything incriminating to say, she'd make it up. And her animosity was no secret to Luther; their relationship was tense and uncomfortable. She wasted time and energy to spread dirt about Luther around the office. Meanwhile, Luther was aware of what she was doing, but his strategy was to make his own case. He focused on other people, and on his goals, giving Connie his attention only when he had to. When they interacted it was short, terse, and to the point. He made sure his relationships with others were healthy, so when her false claims made their way around the office they fell on deaf ears.

His networking paid off. A year later Luther accepted a plum assignment at another station. When he left, he wrote Connie a letter thanking her for making him stronger. Even though it had been a difficult time for him, it was over. He recognized their encounter as an opportunity to learn about himself, and he told her he was grateful to her for being his teacher.

Two years after that, they bumped into each other at a conference. Luther's first thought was to head for the exit when he saw Connie. But she ran to him, threw her arms around him, and thanked him for his letter. She said it had meant a great deal to her.

The tension of the past was gone. Instead of accusing her of making his life miserable, he had welcomed the lessons she brought him. She probably felt guilty that she'd been so cruel to him, and appreciated his lack of hostility. It was as though he had taken her quill and used it to write her a note.

Whether you deal with porcupines or hyenas on a regular basis, one element is always necessary to effectively cope: "helicopter perspective." You must rise above your interactions with them so that you can move beyond your typical reactions to their inane behavior. Understanding a few models will help you do that.

EIGHT

A Model Way of Dealing

Break the Chains

People are predictable only to a certain degree. The point of using this book, of knowing when to let go, of expressing yourself, of making yourself heard, is to create inner freedom. As you know, you aren't going to change difficult people; you can't make them disappear. What you *can* change is you.

Human behavior is not an exact science. What works in one case may not work in another. In fact, what works right now may not work tomorrow, even with the same person. Be armed with a variety of techniques and try another when your first attempt fails. The key to making the next technique work is to realize you *always* have a choice.

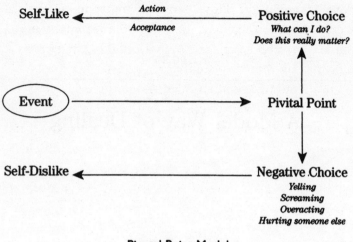

Pivotal Point Model

The Moment of Choice

The moment after an event occurs, you respond. What you may not be aware of is that you've made a choice. Often, it appears as though there is an automatic system that kicks in, but in fact you're really just making choices based on your old habits. The only thing that's automatic is how you fall into your patterns of behavior.

Recognize the moment of choice. This is the pivotal point, the time to change the outcome by asking yourself questions. How am I going to handle this interaction? Negative behavior leads to raised voices, increased blood pressure and adrenaline, and a cycle of self-dislike.

What are your options? How can you align your emotions with reality? How can you move to a level of acceptance? You may not like what's happening, but you can accept it and explore rational options for modifying it or making it more palatable.

Have you ever been stuck in traffic? What is your automatic reaction when you see those blaring brake lights in front of you, knowing they are preventing you from getting to work, home, or a meeting on time? For most people, it's "Oh, sh—." We automatically choose a negative reaction. The pivotal point is a second in time, to which most of us have a patterned negative response. So, after we've finished cussing and waving our arms at other drivers and our blood pressure has shot up, and our immune systems are down, we go into self-dislike. We feel bad that we overreacted, or that we didn't leave soon enough, or take the right route, or live in the right city. But the good news is that we have a choice. We can go back and choose a more positive reaction by asking the question, "What can I do?" This gives us a way of thinking we didn't have before. You can also ask, "Is this worth getting upset over?" Sometimes the answer is yes, but most of the time, it's no. When we ask "What can I do?" we get one of two responses: action or acceptance. We either see or investigate new options or we accept and align ourselves with reality. It doesn't mean you like what's happening; you just accept it. Here's an example of how I applied this concept of aligning oneself with reality:

Alignment

One time while stuck in traffic in Washington, D.C., on my way to an important meeting, I hit the pivotal point. At first I went the negative route and got very upset. But then I began to ask myself, "What can I do?" I asked over and over again. Initially, I felt powerless, but then an idea arose. I jumped out of my car and began to walk around in traffic. Up ahead I saw a car with an antenna on the back of it. I approached the car and signaled for the driver to roll down his window. We greeted each other and I remarked that I had seen the antenna and asked if I could borrow his car phone. He obliged, handed me the phone, and I called to let the others know that I would be late. I hung up and he and I began to talk. We spoke for a little while and exchanged cards. We had lunch a week later. You never know who you're going to meet in traffic. I went back to my car and relaxed. I had done what I could. Now all I could do was accept the situation and wait. Whenever you become aware of the pivotal point, observing yourself and others helps you to remain calm and objective. Becoming a better and bigger observer of yourself automatically makes you a better observer of others.

Observe yourself. Imagine you're watching yourself in an interaction with others. How do you observe yourself? Become neutral; be objective. If you saw a film clip of yourself, would you be embarrassed? Would you wish you had done or said something different? How about the others? Are you really seeing them? Hearing them? Or do you see your own thoughts about them? Wake up to what is really going on. Listen to others without judgment. Put your own importance into the proper perspective. This perspective can stop you from repeating actions that have harmed you in the past.

Becoming an observer also gives you a level of objectivity. By stepping back to examine the situation, you're also giving yourself a window of time. With some visual space, and a pause in time, you can act rationally instead of reacting emotionally.

Road Warriors

Psychologists classify 20 percent of the population as hostile types, for whom minor irritations simmer until they boil. Their aggressiveness often plays out on the road, but driving isn't the problem. It's their reactions to driving that get them in trouble.

Another car drives too slow in the left lane, fails to signal, or travels too close. Suddenly, the hostile driver experiences the urge to duel, guarding his or her piece of the road as territory.

Research reveals that most crashes are caused by drivers who have suffered some kind of personal or professional setback. Their resentment and anger levels are already elevated, and when they get behind the wheel, tempers flare.

Previously we talked about stakes, and about how the amount of risk we're willing to take depends on the context of the relationship. On the road, drivers feel anony-mous, and the stakes are low. Aggressive drivers feel none of the social controls that might inhibit their behavior in the workplace or at a party. They can honk at you, curse you, make rude gestures, and then speed away. They never have to face you or see your reaction. They can be mean without guilt, act without responsibility, and sometimes even cause damage without consequence.

Here's the point: Driving doesn't make someone ag-gressive. Their problems start far from the road. By the same token, your difficult person probably came to you with a high level of agitation. You didn't steer him into acting the way he does; you just happen to be in his path.

Who's Driving Your Emotional Car?

We either assume responsibility for what happens to us or blame others for it. Those who operate from an exter-nal locus of control (ELOC) spend lots of energy making excuses, placing blame, and finding fault with others. They are victims, and they feel that the universe is con-spiring to persecute them and make them miserable. Those who operate from an internal locus of control (ILOC) un-derstand how they influence the ebb and flow of their own lives. They are less interested in perpetrators and more interested in what can be done to meet a challenge.

Your decision to see the world through one of these two windows affects how you behave, what you say, and how

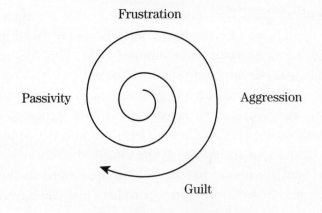

Passive-Aggressive Spiral

you say it. Ask yourself, "Am I driving this car, or am I giving the wheel to someone else?"

Spiraling out of Control

A friend of mine was devastated when she found herself a widow at fifty. Being alone was unfamiliar and frightening, so she decided to find a man right away. She eschewed some popular singles options and went straight to the classified ads.

She answered an ad and agreed to have coffee with the man who placed it. Shortly after they met, she recounted how lovely he'd made her feel, how he showered her with compliments and blotted out the loneliness. But something tickling at the back of her intuition told her maybe it was best not to see him again. She said she had a "funny feeling" about him. But addicts often deny that the things they're addicted to could hurt them, just as my friend ignored her small voice and continued to see him. His attention was her drug, and she was hooked.

He didn't feel that he was getting enough in return for his efforts. When she refused his marriage proposal it pushed his hot button. He took her deep into the woods and held a gun to her head. She managed to calm him down and get herself to safety. Later he begged for her forgiveness and pleaded with her to help him. She agreed to get together with him again. The cycle continued.

He was caught in a passive-aggressive spiral, giving her needs higher priority than his own, and then exploding when he built up enough resentment. To woo her at all costs, he denied his own needs. Resentment built until it erupted like a volcano, aggressive and violent. After his fury was spent, he felt guilty and embarrassed by his outburst. He knelt and begged for forgiveness, driving him back to the beginning of the spiral. She was caught in a web of dependency, relying on his affirmation to bolster her own self-esteem. During this time she continued to call me, insisting that she needed his love and approval to feel good about herself. She was stuck.

Finally she decided to look closely at this situation and how it had escalated to violence and abuse. And she asked herself one pivotal question: "How am I contributing to this relationship and why am I allowing it to continue?" She had given the control of the situation, and her emotions, to him. By changing from an ELOC to an ILOC perspective, she opened up a whole new set of options.

With the help of therapists and the benefit of a little distance, my friend realized how much power she had given up, and how important it was to reclaim it. When she examined herself through the window of ILOC, she gave herself permission to say no to negative or hurtful intrusions into her life. She grew more responsible, and strong enough to decline his invitations. She broke away and today is in a healthier and more fulfilling relationship.

How ELOC and ILOC Act Out

Passive people are quiet. They draw in their shoulders and shrink into themselves, and wait to be recognized. They avoid conflict as well as responsibility, and try to win approval.

Aggressive people are loud. They use their voice and body language to get attention. They need to be right, are very demanding, and put their interests ahead of the interests of others.

Passive and aggressive people have two things in common. They both act out of fear, and they both have an external locus of control. They can't connect what is happening in the present to their own actions, and always believe that they're being taken on a wild ride.

On the other hand, assertive people are calm and confident. They take care of their own needs, but they also consider the needs of others. They mediate and negotiate, finding solutions that require little or no sacrifice. They operate from an internal locus of control, assuming responsibility and acting with respect for themselves and others.

Think of the three types in this way: Passive people wait to be told, aggressive people tell, and assertive people ask.

The Fortune of the Cookie

There is a cookie on the table, and three people sitting around the table want it. One person is passive, one is aggressive, and one is assertive. How do these hungry personalities act?

The passive person gives up the right to the cookie. He supplants his desire for the sake of making the other two happy and earning their approval. The aggressive person assumes she is entitled to the cookie and eats it, even if she just ate a whole box. The assertive person asks the other two if they'd like to share it, thereby getting some for herself while still caring for the others.

Where Does the Sun Rise and Set?

Some people are inclined to think of themselves as the focus of all else, and are very creative when it comes to relating other people's actions to themselves. It's a kind of arrested development. Throughout the early years, children are incapable of thinking beyond themselves. Very young children can't grasp the concept of sharing, because they can't acknowledge that another person has a desire, much less care enough to fulfill that desire. Babies don't even understand that there is a place where they end and their parents begin. For most kids, they really are the center of the world, particularly the world within their own homes.

Part of maturing is accepting one's place within the larger family, then community, then society. But some people are more successful making those leaps than others. Consequently, you may be stuck dealing with someone whose expectation of you is similar to his expectations of his own parents.

Some situations lead us to validate our "I" thinking. When we're uncertain about our relationships, we examine them more carefully for signs and signals of approval or validation. Also, when we do someone a favor or make a gesture we think was especially gracious, we expect more consideration. The person who doesn't return your call invokes much more of your ire if you found her her job or introduced her to her boyfriend.

Fishing Expeditions

Some people, especially sarcastic types, find sport in provoking others. They cast a line, dangle the bait, and if they can reel you in, they've scored. They watch you twist in the net, catching at the mesh, thinking if you flap hard enough they will set you free.

Nate Goes Fishing

MY MOTHER'S FRIEND Nate likes to fish with me. He knows that, like many women, I'm sensitive about my weight, so he likes to push that button and get the response he's looking for. A typical conversation sounds something like this:

"Looks like you've put on a few pounds," he says.

"Oh, be quiet, Nate," I say.

"I see since you started eating meat again you're putting on some weight," he continues.

"Nate, stop talking like that," I insist.

"Yeah, before you know it, we'll have to buy you two seats on the airplane," he persists.

It goes on like this for a while, back and forth, with him attacking me and having his fun. I feel hurt, angry, and frustrated that what I'm doing doesn't silence him.

His first words are like a request for me to swallow that bait, and allow him to swing me up on deck. By responding in a way that furthers the engagement, I'm granting him permission to lure me, and ensnare me. The only way to keep myself out of the frying pan is to spit out the hook. One day I finally realized what was going on—that this is entertainment for him—and then I was able to break the cycle. I got up, left the room, changed the subject, and turned on the television. I had to give him the message that his attacks would not merit a response.

I had to be the one to stop it. I couldn't *make* him stop, but I could chew through that fishing net and set myself free. In the past, Nate was a regular button pusher, but now I'm able to move beyond his childish irritations. It takes two to tango, and two to tangle. I'm getting out of the boat.

Personalities come in all shapes, sizes and flavors. They have different names and dysfunctions. Whatever types of personalities you're dealing with, the important point to remember is that they are doing the best they can considering what they've got to work with (sometimes it's not much), given their background, experiences, and perspective. Understanding and defining their limitations increases your ability to stand back, understand, and more important, respond. Now that you know who they are and what they do, the question is: What do you do with them? How do you tango or tangle? What part do you play in encouraging their difficultness and how can you pull yourself out of the situation forever?

NINE

How to Spot Trouble from Across the Room

Patterns of Relationships

Why does Ruth get along with Sam, but Sam doesn't get along with you? Is Sam the problem, or are you? Is there something about the nature of your encounters that has biased you against one another, or did something specific happen to taint the relationship?

Human interactions are like dances. One person stands, extends a hand, and invites the other person to participate in a series of steps timed to an external rhythm. Sometimes the hand is slapped away, other times accepted reluctantly. But the pattern of the dance flows from the roles established at the outset.

Here are some examples of how this dance can play out:

- You push my button and I'll push yours (the most popular): The ultimate "let's dance" pattern.

- You push my button and I'll ignore you: A quest for attention.

- I'll push your button (or just try to get a response) and you ignore me: The I'm-so-much-better-than-you-are routine.

We can identify several different patterns and the behaviors associated with each. Do any of these scenarios describe your relationship with your difficult person?

- The master yells at and abuses the slave. The slave accepts it, but builds resentment.

- The saboteur is a backstabber. She withholds information and spreads gossip. She commits subterfuge, undermining you. She is sneaky and underhanded.

- The chaser is offensive. The moving target is defensive.

- The lapdog is completely passive. He has no boundaries. Approval from the "master" is paramount.

Hot and Cool Buttons

Hot buttons are things that really drive you crazy. Your annoyances. Your pet peeves. Your triggers.

Cool buttons are the things you'd like to have more of.

Often, people don't know what they want, but they know what they don't want. Concentrating on what you don't want leaves you living with the hot buttons, and doesn't move you forward.

Hot button: "When people interrupt me." Cool button: "When people listen carefully to what I say and wait for me to finish my thought." Hot button: "Incessant talking." Cool button: "Concise, active conversation." Hot button: "Complaints." Cool button: "Solutions."

See the difference? Now the trick is letting other people know what our hot and cool buttons are.

Opposites Attract

In the 1970s, Thomas Harris, author of *I'm OK, You're OK*, popularized the theory of transactional analysis. When one participant in a transaction assumes a certain role, the other participant automatically assumes the opposing role. When a boss acts like a parent, the employee acts like a child. This cycle is easy to fall into, but hard to break.

The person in the authority role must talk to the subordinate more like one adult to another. If the subordinate is treated like an adult, with respect and acceptance, he is less likely to act childishly.

Another way to break the pattern is for the employee to think of herself more as an adult, and to respond in a mature way. It will become impossible for the boss to act like a parent once the child has left the scene.

A boss can say: "You'd better have that project ready by Friday, or else!" speaking in the parental role; or he can say: "What's your schedule like? Can you get that finished up by Friday?" speaking from the adult perspective. The best way to transform the role of parent or child is to realize that the boss is looking for a partner (with whom to tango or tangle) and to respond with neutral questions from the adult's role, such as "What's our next step?" The adult-adult dynamic will give you more options and power.

Make My Day

MY FRIEND JILL was feeling down, so I sent her a dozen roses, assuming it would make her feel better. But Jill's ex-boyfriend used to send her roses all the time, and seeing them reminded her of their messy split. The flowers had the opposite effect of what I'd intended. I needed to rethink my gesture. Did I fail? Did I do something bad because I didn't "make" her feel better? Of course not. The good thing I had done was send the flowers. Her reaction to them had nothing to do with me, nor could I really influence it.

Show Me Your Buttons, and I'll Push Them

I can't trigger something in you that isn't already there. The button has to exist for me to push it. Therefore, no one can "make" you angry, upset, happy, etc. We tend to use this language often, but every time we say someone has "made" us feel something, we're giving up power. What people do is invite us to participate and we accept their invitations with our reactions, words, and behaviors.

If you do something that upsets me, I need to tell you because it feels good to get it off my chest, not because I expect you to be different. If I have the perspective that expressing anger will cause you to do what I want you to do, surely I will be disappointed. We have to express our concerns, anger, and frustration because of *our* need to say something about it first, and for change to happen as a result of what we say second. Being heard is what changes the feeling.

We don't create reaction, we activate it. Our actions are like throwing a match on hot charcoals, doused with lighter fluid. The more we are aware of our own reactions to these situations, the less affected we will be. We will begin to see difficult people as a reflection of our own state, our own ability to be rattled, and how determined we are to be unshaken. One of the tools that will continue to assist us in this is language. Now that we understand the dynamics of what's happening in an interaction with difficult people, the question becomes: What do we say to them and how do we say it?

Thought into Action

TAKE THREE STRIPS of red paper, and on each one write something that sets you off. Be specific. Begin each with: "It really drives me crazy when someone . . ." Does your difficult person routinely commit these infractions?

On three strips of green paper, write your cool buttons. Each one should be an antidote to a hot button. "I'd really like it if . . ." What can you tell people to do that would make you happier?

Figure out a way to make people aware of your hot and cool buttons. Speak about them indirectly. If someone is making you wait, you could say "This is my hot button. I hate it when people make me wait." Or approach them during a neutral conversation when your hot buttons aren't being pushed. You could even post the green and red papers near your desk. If you work on a team, it would be helpful to talk about what those hot and cool buttons are, so people know how to avoid them and when they're being pushed.

PART THREE

Tools and Recipes

What you think upon grows. Whatever you allow to occupy your mind you magnify in your own life. Whether the subject of your thought be good or bad, the law works and the condition grows. Any subject that you keep out of your mind tends to diminish in your life, because what you do not use atrophies.

—*Emmet Fox,* Around the Year with Emmet Fox

TEN

Talking Your Way Out of a Paper Bag

Language Is Action

As Julio Olalla, a noted coach in the areas of organizational development, says: Language is action. When we speak, we generate our reality and generate our future. Everything that happens in life is generated from language. If I say I am disgustingly overweight, that assessment will cause me to act in a particular way. Because I say I'm fat, I'm going to skip a party on Saturday night. I don't feel comfortable, I'm unhappy about the way I look, and no one is going to want to talk to me. The assessment that I've made is a block. I have just closed a door to my future.

Another example: If after we have an argument I tell you I'm really sorry, I then ask you to please forgive me. You accept my apology, and say, "I forgive you." At that moment, the animosity stops and our relationship begins anew—a relationship of possibility, of things we can do together. We've exorcised the demons that plagued us. If I'm truly sorry, and you can truly forgive, then those words create a context for our relationship to continue, and form a new perspective.

In fact, when people weather a stormy episode or repair a rift, they often feel closer and more tightly bonded. Learning to trust and forgive adds another dimension to a relationship. Idyllic, problem-free relationships are either very superficial or very young. The most solid connections between people are not those that exist without problems, but rather those that have faced problems and resolved them.

Speech in Context

What Are You Doing?

The way we respond to people has a great deal to do with our relationship. We'll speak differently to our boss than to a colleague, a sibling, or a friend. We also speak differently depending on the last time we spoke with someone. If a friend calls and asks, "What are you doing?" you tell her what you're doing right now. If a friend you haven't seen in ten years calls and asks the same question, you talk about the major events of your life. Who is asking and what they're asking determines your answer. The situation creates the context.

You also act differently with different people. When your father calls, the child in you may appear. With your spouse, you become the partner. But what about difficult people? Who are you when you encounter them, and how does that affect the way you behave?

Language Creates the Perception

Eskimos make different distinctions about snow than most mainland Americans do. We have one phenomenon we know as snow. But they have so much of it, and it's such a huge factor in their daily lives, that they speak about it differently. They use different words for light snow and heavy snow, for wet snow and dry snow. They also have distinctions in whiteness. They see snow differently because they define snow differently. In this way, language creates, and reinforces, the perception.

Understanding these nuances helps create more connected conversations. This is why people who are from the same city or background often have a stronger connection. The language, cadence, and slang of that background can connect or divide us. Sometimes situations are difficult because of the lack of understanding in the conversation. So what kinds of conversations are you having, and how can you steer them in the direction you want them to go?

Conversations

Whether we realize it or not, we're constantly having conversations, and everything that happens in our lives is the result of a conversation. This book is the result of a conversation between me and an editor, between me and a literary agent, between the agent and a publisher. Maybe you're reading it because you talked about it with a friend or the clerk in the bookstore.

Empires are built and destroyed from conversations. Presidents are elected, criminals sentenced to die. Conversations are the very basis of our social structure. When we realize that we can't have anything without conversations—not marriages, not cars, not jobs, not homes—then we begin to examine what we're really saying. We give our speaking more value and more consideration.

We also communicate through tone and body language, which either reinforces or contradicts what our words are conveying. Without the benefit of a soft voice or a reassuring smile, critical words seem much more harsh.

In an office many conversations take place in writing, whether they be memos, e-mail messages, faxes, or scrawls on a sticky note. The formal letter allows for a certain amount of distance, and the writer usually chooses his or her words more carefully.

Everything stems from conversations, so think about the conversations you have. Do they generate possibilities and result in action? Are you making offers? Are you complaining or arguing? Those don't go anywhere. You can have problem-oriented conversations or ones that are more creative and move you ahead.

There are four kinds of conversations. The first kind is **stories and assessments**. People like to have these conversations, but they don't always like to be the subject of them. Such conversations can be gossip about other people. These conversations can also be for pure fun and for the sake of the relationship. For instance, the other night I called a friend just to say hello. I wanted to find out how he was and what was up in his life, and to chat for a few minutes. Nothing more, nothing less. In our exchange he reported stories and assessments, not so much about others, but about what was happening with him, how he assessed what was happening, and what was next. Sharing. Bonding. Exchanging experiences. They don't necessarily lead to action, but they ultimately strengthen the connection. They build the context in which possibilities for action can take place. They enrich our lives, help us feel understood, and support us in having other types of conversations in the world.

The second type is conversation for **future discussion**. These are short and are usually built around scheduling and timing. "When can we meet to discuss this?" is a typical question that would open that conversation. Sometimes a meeting or a dialogue might end with this kind of interaction. It's like a diving board to the next interaction.

The third type is conversation for **expanding ideas**. "How might we work together?" is a question that would open this kind of conversation. These conversations usually stem from requests, and often take the form of brainstorming. They explore opportunities. They're creative and purposeful. A possibility can be either an action or further discussion. Such conversations move the participants forward and set the stage for change.

The fourth type is conversation for **action**. This is where deals and negotiations take place. Parties agree to do things and to take responsibility for pieces of a task. In these conversations, commitments are made and change is set in motion. Most of the conversations at the workplace, whether it is between a secretary and a boss or two CEOs, revolve around this kind of conversation. It's what you get paid to do.

Thought into Action

BE AWARE OF the kinds of conversations you get into. Take a day and see if you can define the types of conversations you find yourself engaging in. If you find yourself discussing something negative, talking unkindly about someone else, or in a circular argument, stop. Try changing the subject to a more productive one, or remove yourself from it. Concentrate on making your conversations more action oriented and using words that propel you to a better understanding.

Assess the conversations of the people you like the most. What do they speak about? How do they speak about it? What words do they use? What do they focus on?

A Deeper Understanding of the Difficult Person

Understanding the difficult person reduces your irritation level, makes you feel better, and puts you in a better state to deal with those situations when they arise.

When a person is behaving in a difficult way, causing problems, picking fights, or being passive, he is, in that moment, dysfunctional. He is doing only what he can, given what he's got. As far as he can see, his choices are limited. It's as though he's stuck in a corner, and can't even see the exit door.

The authors of *Executive EQ* remind us that "feelings are facts to the person experiencing them. In many situations, a single calm comment can help diffuse emotional overreaction and promote creative solution finding."

Sometimes we get angry at people because we think they intend to be malicious, but in fact they really just don't know any better. In most cases, given their past, their dysfunction, and the choices they think they have, they react from a place of fear. They feel helpless, and there is nothing else for them to do.

Human Laundry Baskets

What do you do when there's no place to put your anger? Sometimes we use difficult people as scapegoats for unexpressed or unresolved feelings. Rather than air our "dirty laundry," we store resentments and then use a person's difficultness as an excuse to toss our anger at them.

Is your response to your difficult person exaggerated by lingering discontent with yourself or someone else? Judge how appropriate your reactions are. If they seem out of proportion, you may be looking for a place to unload your soiled feelings.

Imagine you're putting the finishing touches on your brand new boat, and as you sit there, bobbing on the water with the sun on your back, a speedboat blazes across the lake. You yell, you flail your arms, but it keeps coming. You dive into the water, just as another boat plows into yours and smashes it to bits.

You're so angry that your face flushes and your heart pounds in your ears. You swear revenge against whoever rammed you, until you notice that no one was on the boat. Suddenly your fury evaporates, and while you may still be upset that your boat is destroyed, you realize that this was an accident and not a deliberate attack. Your anger, a moment ago flaring, now dissipates. There's no one to target, no one to give it to or justify it with. Sometimes all difficult people do is give us an outlet for anger that already belongs to us. So how do we redirect this anger that may already be present? The answer: Focus it inside ourselves instead of toward someone else.

Verbal Aikido

IN MARTIAL ARTS, practitioners of aikido don't brace themselves against a person coming toward them. Instead, they use the momentum of their attacker to thwart their advance. They guide and redirect the oncoming energy, rather than meet it with a solid block. In doing so, the person moves forward and down. Here are some examples of how to translate this physical principle into a verbal one.

Using Verbal Akido Techniques
Your Objective: To open the option door as wideas possible and speak about what the difficult person *can* do rather than what he/she can't. These phrases work especially well in a customer-service context or when someone wants something from you and you can't or don't want to give it to them.

What to Say:
- Here are your options . . .
- What I can give/tell you is . . .
- What you *can* do is . . .
- Which would you rather have . . .
- Give me some specifics so that I can see how to help you.
- Let's talk about this for a minute.
- Have you tried . . .
- You make the choice.

What these phrases do is open and redirect the conversation where you want it to go. While the person may not get the solution he/she wants, he does get some other possibility. That's what you're offering: options.

Become aware of what you are presently saying to customers and colleagues. See if you find yourself saying things from this column:

What Not to Say:
- No Comment.
- I can't answer that (no more response).
- Maybe. Maybe not.
- You are an idiot.
- Ma'am, I understand, but . . .
- It's not company policy.
- You have no choice.

Using this philosophy, practice verbal aikido. Employ techniques and tactics that allow your difficult people to glance off you, and absorb the impact themselves. Rather than be a wall they slam into, be a gate they swing open and go through. The sheer force, when it fails to meet the resistance, will cause them to lose control and stumble.

Listening: Do You Hear What I Hear?

Hearing is a biological phenomenon; listening is an interpretation. I can say a word, and two people can hear it, but each may interpret it differently.

Suppose three people are working together. One says, "When we finish working, we're going to take a walk in the woods." The other two hear the same statement, but while one thinks it would be great to get a little fresh air and stretch her legs, the other thinks about her allergies, and how miserable it'll be to drag herself along a pollen-ridden woodland path. Just because you heard it one way, doesn't mean that's how it was meant, nor does it mean that others got the same message.

Can I Get a Witness?

Does a tree falling in a forest make a noise if there is no one there to hear it? This old riddle suggests that without an ear to experience the sound, there is no sound generated. By the same token, the listener in any conversation gives the speaker legitimacy.

You honor a person by listening to him or her, as a king grants an audience to someone he feels worthy of his attention. Your listening presence gives the speaker power.

How you listen to someone is a reflection of your fundamental relationship with that person. Think of someone you feel you can really talk to. Do you feel comfortable talking to him because he lets you ramble on and doesn't interrupt? Or is it because he really listens to you, and says things that show he understands and cares about what you're saying? Listening is more than hearing; it's following your thoughts, showing respect for your point of view, and showing acceptance for you as a person.

If you doubt the power of listening, think of its flip side. What happens when someone ignores you? See how Laurie feels when she isn't acknowledged. How would you handle it?

The Cold Shoulder

WHEN LAURIE WAS young, her mother would express anger and disapproval by ignoring her. To Laurie, there was no greater punishment. She would plead with her mother to take away her privileges, cut her off from her friends, even hit her, as long as she stopped the silent treatment. She would beg, "Moooom, talk to me." She did annoying things to catch her mother's attention, but she continued to be ignored.

Without being able to engage her mother in conversation, Laurie felt immobilized. She had no mechanisms for dealing with her guilt, and could not resolve the situation or serve penance. Until she found a way to break her mother's stony silence, or her mother let go of it on her own, they were locked in a hopeless web of hurt. Laurie began to shut down and eventually needed psychiatric care. By the time she was an adult, it became difficult for her to hold a job, have a relationship, and function effectively in the world. She eventually was checked into an institution and has stayed there until this day.

Not speaking can say more than yelling. But when difficult people ignore us, is it more about them or us?

Personalizing and Depersonalizing

Stuff happens. People don't speak to us the way we would like them to, or perhaps they don't speak at all. But how do we take it? Let's look at some typical examples of what people might say or do and how we interpret their actions.

Event: Mary doesn't speak to you.

Your interpretation: "She hates me."

What may have really happened: Mary just got some bad news and is self-absorbed.

Event: Fred doesn't answer your call.

Your interpretation: "He's trying to get rid of me."

What may have really happened: Fred got called out of town and didn't even get your message.

Event: Joe doesn't answer your question.

Your interpretation: "He's ignoring me."

What may have really happened: He didn't hear you. Or he's afraid to admit he doesn't have an answer.

What you're doing with these kinds of interpretations is called *personalizing*. We often assume the actions of others are related to something we've done, when they probably have nothing to do with us at all.

By the time you encounter that person again, you're so angry because of what you assumed that the relationship has already rung a sour note. You think the explanation you've created is the truth and that it can't be altered. Convinced that this person hates you, you have to hate her back. You've taken an action out of context and formed an assessment, and now you're obligated to collect further evidence to support your determination. So much of our thinking springs from the "I" that everything becomes personal. If "I" am the center of the universe, then "I" must be the cause of this, and everything, no matter what else might be involved, relates back to "me."

So, how do you handle it? Assume, unless you get evidence to the contrary, that it's about the other person. When you get information indicating you've done something, then take responsibility for what you can, go into solution, and move on. The less you focus on "whodunit," and the more you focus on how to move on, the happier you will be.

Thought into Action

CHANGE THE CONVERSATION you have with yourself to take the focus off the difficult person and put it on you. Here's a sample of how a conversation like this might unfold. The "cynical you" is the part that perpetuates the cycle of negative thinking toward difficult people. The "diffuser you" offers a new way of thinking. The next time you're faced with a difficult person, have a conversation like this inside your head.

Cynical You: "Oh, God here comes the boss again. I thought I'd gotten her off my back for the day."

Diffuser You: "Relax. We've got it all under control. She's going to walk out of here without setting me off, and she won't even know what I've done."

Cynical You: "Are you kidding? She's been driving me crazy all day, asking questions, demanding things, yelling her orders. The sound of her footsteps is making my stomach knot."

Diffuser You: "Breathe. Let the air flow through your body. Remind yourself that there is nothing out there to be upset about, that it's her trip and she can have it. You are in charge of what you think, feel, and say. Everything's cool."

Then the boss enters screaming.

Diffuser You (to the boss in a neutral tone): "Specifically, what needs to be done right now?"

The boss screams her commands.

Diffuser You: "I will handle that by five this afternoon. Anything else?"

The boss leaves, confused.

Whenever you change your behavior patterns, people don't know what to make of it. At first they will insist on maintaining their own behavior patterns, hoping to keep up the familiar game. Then they will probably be a bit confused. Ultimately they will change in response to you. Chances are, the boss won't continue her bellowing. Meanwhile, you are directing your inner and outer conversations so that you get new thoughts and action. This way of thinking changes the outcome of one or all your frustrating interactions.

Are Your Ears Plugged?

How you listen determines your relationships. We put a lot of emphasis in our society on what we say, but listening is at least as important. How do you listen to your difficult person? Do you stare at the floor, tap your toes, and wait impatiently for her to finish? Are you busy thinking about what you'll say next? Hard as it may be, try honoring her with more of your interest, and repeating some of her phrases to show that you're really listening. Look her in the eye, and don't allow anything to distract you while she speaks. See if this change in your listening effects a change in her speaking. Maybe she's been shouting to capture your attention.

. . . Or Do They Need to Be?

On the other hand, you may be dealing with someone who doesn't merit your listening. If your difficult person complains endlessly and tries to draw you into unpleasantness you don't need to be involved in, the best strategy is to ignore him, or keep your conversation short. In the same way that you feel frustrated and unable to accomplish your goal, the complainer will ultimately recognize that he isn't getting what he wants from you, and he will eventually give up. Since your goal is to reward the behavior you want to see repeated, don't reward behavior that isn't moving the conversation forward.

The Electronic Byte

Sometimes cyberspace is an alternative place for your interactions. But, if you choose this mode of communication, beware. People who use e-mail view it as a more casual mode of conversation, and often dash off notes without much thought. Without the nonverbal signals conveyed by tone of voice and posture, words can seem severe.

Amy worked for a magazine that relied on information from Marti's department for its editorial copy. An error made its way into the database and ultimately into the magazine. Amy was embarrassed when several readers called to point out the mistake, so she e-mailed a note to Marti, Marti's team, the magazine staff, and others in the company who used the information for other purposes.

What she had intended as a gentle notice to watch for inaccuracies ended up sounding like a strident condemnation of Marti's co-workers and the integrity of their work. Had Amy spoken the words herself, she could have toned it down with her body language and her approach. Her ability to distribute the critique so easily to so many people only made matters worse.

What Does It Mean to Them?

People don't pay attention to your intention; they pay attention to your behavior, the sum of your words, tone, body language, and action. What you mean to do or say is not nearly as relevant as how you act, so make sure what you do is consistent with what you mean.

Rear Offense

I WENT UP to a friend at a party and poked her on the lower back as a greeting. She became very angry and wouldn't talk to me. I was doing what I thought was a friendly thing, but I'd upset her sensibilities in some way. When I saw her reaction, I apologized. I wanted to discuss it, but she was so upset she wouldn't talk to me.

It wouldn't have been productive for me to defend myself. The fact is that I upset her and I needed to deal with her feelings, not argue the rightness or wrongness of my actions. After I apologized and tried to discuss it with her, I saw that my attempts to reconcile were futile. I let go. A year later she called to talk as if nothing had happened. At that point I didn't care.

Actions Plus Words Speak Loudest

Both words and actions communicate for us, but one without the other doesn't carry enough weight. When words are coupled with actions, they produce the most significant effects. The words and the actions must be consistent. If they contrast, one diminishes the impact of the other. If you say something to someone, back it up with appropriate actions.

Some words are also actions; they cause one situation to end and another to begin. Words such as "I'm sorry" create new realities.

Thought into Action

WRITING IS MORE easily controlled than speaking. You have the luxury of changing what you said, or withdrawing it altogether, before it's too late. If you need to put something in writing, build in enough time for a "cooling off" period. Write it, put it away, and come back to it later when your intention has faded slightly and you can reread what you wrote more objectively. Let the emotion of that moment pass, then really look at the words on the page and listen to what they say on their own, without the sound of your own voice saying them in your mind.

Think about the implications of what you write. Can it be interpreted any other way? What would your body language and tone be like if you were saying these words in person? Is the same message coming through without the benefit of your presence?

A Power Lunch

I went out for brunch with my family to celebrate Mother's Day. We all sat in the smoking section of the restaurant, with the smokers clustered at one end. Since I don't smoke and don't like to smell it while I'm eating, I chose a spot on the other end.

My mother and her friend Norman were in the smoking section of the table, and they wanted me to join them. He beckoned to me as I prepared to sit, and I told him firmly that I'd rather sit at the other end of the table. Then, as if I were a child and he the controlling parent, he said, "Get your fat butt over here and sit down right now!"

His words infuriated me. Anger rode through me like a wild roller coaster. I wanted not only to speak, but to scream and yell back. Instead I counted to ten and was silent as a stone. And that pause was a powerful tool. For one thing, it gave me the opportunity to assess the situation and respond in a rational way. For another, it made him wonder what was going to come next, instead of expecting us to fall into an old and familiar pattern.

Then I said in a firm tone, "If I have given you any indications that it is OK to talk to me like that, I want you to know that it wasn't my intention. I don't ever want you to talk to me like that again." Norman was flabbergasted and silenced by my firm honesty. He didn't know what to say.

When I did sit, it was in my original seat, at the opposite end of the table from Norman and my mother. Had

> ## *Thought into Action*
>
> IN YOUR NEXT encounter with difficult behavior, re-
> think your intention. What do you want to achieve? When
> you've got an answer, declare it to yourself unequivocally. The
> intention shouldn't be about winning, but about reprogramming
> your responses. Try these declarations: "I'm going to handle
> this with strength and poise." "A solution will present itself."
> "I intend to find a solution with ease and grace." "There may
> be a solution I don't see yet."

I told him to stop insulting me, and then sat with him, he
could have interpreted my actions as permission to continue his abusive behavior.

I could tell that I had made an impression on him, and
that he felt remorseful. I realized that this technique
worked for a few reasons. First, although he addressed me
as if I were a child, I did not respond like one. I was not
overly emotional, hurt, or defensive. Second, I stated simply that what he did was not acceptable, and even took
some responsibility for possibly leading him to believe that
it was. And third, I backed it up with action.

I know this situation had an impact on Norman. The
next day we went out to lunch and *he* insisted we sit in
the nonsmoking section. I knew that in his own twisted
way, he was letting me know that he got the message.

As you can see from this example, language can hurt
or heal. While body language and tone are crucial to a

conversation, the words themselves are of great importance.

Sticks and Stones

Words can, and do, hurt us, despite the old adage. Speaking is acting, and a sharp word can cause pain as surely as a sharpened sword. Words must be measured carefully; once spoken, they cannot be retrieved. And all too often, unkind words make their way back to the subject. Even if you're talking to an impartial party and you think you're speaking in confidence, ask yourself what would happen if the person you're talking about heard what you were saying. Remember too, that he will hear it thirdhand, out of context, and you won't be there to defend your words before they're interpreted. Further, insult is added to injury. What you said is bad enough; the fact that you were gossiping about someone makes matters worse.

Of course the speaker can ask the subject for forgiveness, and relationships can move past hurtful words. But once spoken, they exist; they become part of an intangible reality, and they can't be erased.

It's easy to think that names will never hurt, but we know the painful power of words. Wars within families and between countries have been started with the wrong words, and can be ended with the right words. In any relationship the power of words pulls us together or pushes us apart.

The Broken Pyramid

A GROUP OF high school students met in Gabe's office every week to talk about the realities of teen life. The kids got along really well, but Andy was targeted as an outcast and became the subject of a lot of ribbing. The kids didn't intend to be mean, and they didn't think Andy minded the laughs they got at his expense. In fact, they thought he enjoyed the attention.

During one of the sessions, the group launched a string of Andy jokes. The laughter built, and even those that usually didn't participate joined in. Suddenly Gabe smashed a ceramic pyramid on the floor, sending shards skittering across the room.

Everyone stared at their shoes in stunned silence, feeling embarrassed and a little scared by this otherwise placid man's action. Gabe picked up the pieces of the pyramid, which someone had made for him in art studio, and examined them. "I can glue these back together," he said softly, "but there will be holes where tiny pieces are missing. I could have the person who made it for me make another one. I could leave it the way it is. But it will never be the same. And that is the way it is with words that hurt. Once you say these words, this person will never be the same again. They have an impact. They cannot be undone."

Come Together or Come Apart

Whenever you speak, you're either unifying or separating. Separateness is a big issue for difficult people, in part because they are motivated by feelings of alienation. But your exchanges with them probably reinforce the separateness, much in the way that two negative magnets will repel. The degree to which people unite or separate is subtle, but with difficult people the distance is much more pronounced. You polarize on opposite sides, taking up positions of offense and defense.

Moving toward union doesn't mean abandoning your opinions and deferring to the difficult person. Rather, it's a way of making your point clear without causing separation. By changing to phrases that encourage union, you stop making negative assessments about him as a human being. Focus on one particular area of disagreement rather than condemn him and his whole thought system. What words can you use to acknowledge his opinion, but still express your own?

To be right, to hold onto ego, to maintain the difficulty, is to stay separate. Maybe there's a reason for staying separate. Do you like having this person to complain about? Will you betray an ally if you give up this struggle? Are you prepared to have these relationships be different?

Furniture Friction

I WENT SHOPPING for an armoire with my best friend. She excitedly took me to a new store that she had discovered. On the way, she casually mentioned that she would also like to find an armoire for herself. When we got to the store, she found one that she thought would be perfect for me. She called me over to look at it and I loved it at first sight. I said, "This is perfect." She looked at it. She looked at me. I looked at her. I looked at it. The two of us did a dance around the piece.

The salesman asked if he should put it on hold, and my friend said, "Yes, you should, because I like it too. One of us has to have this." I looked at her quizzically, as if to ask, "What do you mean?" and she continued, "but we'll have to fight about it first."

My body tensed, and we immediately pulled away from each other. "What do you mean, you like it too?" I demanded to know.

"Remember, in the car when I mentioned that I was looking for an armoire?" she reminded me. "Well, that one would be perfect for me."

"Then it was stupid for you to call my attention to it. Why did you call me over and say it was perfect for me if you wanted it for yourself?" I shouted. She responded loudly, "Because I was helping you shop and I didn't think about myself until after I called your attention to it."

Despite this conversation, we continued to shop. We sparred over this one-of-a-kind piece, while trying to interest each other in different armoires. But between curt sentences like, "Why don't *you* take *that* one?" there were moments of icy silence.

When the day ended, neither of us had claimed the prize, nor had we found any other to substitute. At her house that evening, I realized I couldn't enjoy owning it even if I had "won" it; every time I looked at it I knew I'd be reminded of the animosity it had caused between us. I finally said, "You know, I've been thinking. I've decided that the armoire would look better in your place. You can have it." That moment, when I let go, the relationship dynamic shifted and we moved away from our separation, back toward our union and our friendship. She responded, "I don't know. I think it might look better in your place." We both decided to sleep on it.

The next day she told me she didn't really want it, she just wanted to know that she could have it. She was testing my loyalty, pushing to see how much the boundaries of our relationship would tolerate. As long as we were locked in battle, there was no place for us to go. No movement toward union was possible until one of us gave up an end of the struggle.

I also could have averted the separation altogether. Had I seen the argument coming, I could have said, "I forgot that you were also looking for an armoire, so why don't we just keep this one in mind and continue looking?" With this I could have redirected the conversation, created more possibilities for solution, and let the issue of that particular piece of furniture die. Later that month, my friend wound up picking out another armoire for me, even more beautiful than the first.

Thought into Action

MENTALLY REPLAY AN encounter with your difficult person, and think about the words each of you used. Were they words that brought you together, left you at the same level of unproductive distance, or pushed you further apart?

Use the chart that follows to see how words of separateness can be exchanged for words of union.

Words or Statements That Cause Separation (*speaks about the past/ wrongs*)	**Alternatives for Unity** (*speaks about the future/ solutions*)
"You don't do this."	*"We can work together on that."*
"You're wrong."	*"I have a different take on that."*
"That's stupid. My idea is better."	*"That's a possibility. I have an idea to add to that."*
"Why did you do it like that?"	*"What do you think about doing it this way?"*
"You never . . ."	*"It would be great if . . ."*
"You always . . ."	*"You may be right . . ."*
	"I've noticed . . ."
"You better . . ."	*"What would work better is . . ."*
"It's your problem."	*"Let's talk about the solution."*
"If you hadn't . . ."	*"In the future . . ."*

Questions

We're so trained to seek answers that we find it very uncomfortable to ask questions. Confusion comes in the questioning stage, when the answers don't come easily, or they aren't clear. We're very focused on having the answers and being right. We don't want to spend any time with the questions; we want the answer now.

Arrogance is a sign of ignorance. The more significant you think you are, the less open to change and learning you will be. People who think they know it all really know very little. The more you learn, the more you realize how much you don't know.

Many people panic in the face of unanswered questions. But questioning is the basis of change, and of growth. Don't be afraid of questions. If you can master uncertainty, you can start to see how questions offer you something positive: the opportunity for learning. On your quest for answers, you'll find many chances to grow and enrich your life. Start thinking of questions as a bridge to awareness, rather than a chasm into which you might fall.

Fill 'Er Up!

If confusion and questions frustrate you, you will feel helpless, and less likely to move toward a solution. To move forward we need some GAS in our engine. Here are three types of questions we can ask people:

Gathering questions: These questions are ideal with many types of difficult people because they often clarify situations and help them to feel more important in the process. When they feel more important, their idiosyncrasies are less likely to emerge. Gathering questions are nonthreatening by nature, so you incur little defensiveness and anger when you use them. Examples: "Can you tell me about . . . ?" "I'm confused. Could you clarify . . . ?" "How long have you been . . . ?"

Association questions: These questions cause pain or pleasure. They cause the person to think about the consequences of his or her behavior. Examples: "What are we risking by doing it this way?" "What price are we paying for holding off?" "What are we gaining by doing this?"

Solution questions: These questions redirect the person's thinking toward solutions. Examples: "What if we were to . . ." "How about combining two elements of our proposal?"

Thought into Action

WHEN YOU QUESTION someone, use phrases like: "I'm wondering about . . ." "I'm confused about . . ." "I'm curious about . . ." Avoid accusatory statements like: "Why did you do it like that?" In fact, you should probably stay away from "why" altogether in your questions. It puts people on the defensive.

Tone and body language are equally important in finding answers. "*What* the hell were you *thinking?*" carries a critically different message than "What was your thinking on this decision?" Leave profanity and condemnations out of your questions. Try at least one of these types of questions on your difficult people in the next forty-eight hours. Make a note of the results you get. How does being aware of the types of questions you are asking change the answers you get?

Requests

The way we approach people, and how we are approached, has a great deal of influence on how they react or how we react and whether we can really communicate with one another. When we make a request, we often fear that we'll come across as too demanding. Instead of being direct, we'll phrase it as more of a suggestion: "It would be great if you could . . ." This implies it would be exceptional if they do, but still acceptable if they don't.

Formal requests are made up of five basic elements:

- The speaker (the one making the request, and the one who will judge the final product)

- The listener (the person expected to fulfill the request)

- The future action (*what* the speaker wants to see happen, by *when*)

- The conditions of satisfaction (the yardstick by which the speaker will evaluate the outcome)

- A shared background of obviousness (that you both know what you're talking about)

If communications break down, chances are we left an element out.

Most requests are very straightforward. Suppose you (the speaker) ask me (the listener) to hand you a pen (the action). In this case, I can assume you want the pen right now. When the pen is in your hand, you'll feel I've met the conditions of satisfaction.

Do you always know what will make you feel satisfied? Do you always define those conditions when you make requests? This element is the most difficult, since we don't always know what will meet or disappoint our expectations until we evaluate the outcome. Further, we often assume the listener thinks enough like us to do it the way we want.

Requests in the Marketplace

In *Executive EQ*, Robert K. Cooper and Ayman Sawaf cite the work of University of Texas marketing professor Robert Peterson, whose research indicates that an emotional link must form between a businessperson and his or her customer. Without that relationship, customers will probably go elsewhere. Quality, price, and service are the minimum requirements; competitiveness is based on the ability of everyone, from the boss down, to establish a connection with customers. Customers are more comfortable making requests within the context of a relationship, and are more likely to expect satisfaction from the outset of the business transaction. But how do we know when we are satisfied?

Thought into Action

Is THERE SOMETHING you aren't getting that you'd like to have? Try asking for it directly. Before you do, think what specifically you'd like to see happen, when you'd like it done by, and what you would consider satisfactory.

It seems simplistic, but we're sometimes reluctant to state our desires plainly. What are your conditions of satisfaction? Label and articulate them.

Conditions of Satisfaction

In a restaurant, it's pretty clear what will meet your expectations, and what won't. If you ask for bread, it should be fresh and arrive promptly. You should have butter, and a knife to spread it with. There shouldn't be any ants in it. People generally agree what basics will satisfy them in a restaurant, depending on the restaurant. You don't expect filet mignon at McDonald's.

When you go to a restaurant, they're making a promise to you. Usually it's not spoken or written anywhere, but nevertheless they promise to deliver a certain level of service that will meet your conditions of satisfaction. When people say they went to a good restaurant, what they're really saying is that the dining experience met or exceeded their expectations.

One of the major breakdowns at the workplace is that people don't articulate their conditions of satisfaction. Sometimes it's because they don't know what they are. Sometimes it's because they haven't thought about them. Defining them when you make a request will not only make it more likely that your concerns are met, but that the other party will feel successful as well. Here's what results when the conditions of satisfaction are unclear . . .

To Staple or Not to Staple, That Is the Question

MARCIA ASKS THE department assistant to print a three page document and bring it to her. When Joe hands her the report, she stares at it in disbelief. "Why aren't the pages stapled?" she asks. "Don't you see how easily the pages will be separated, and how quickly they can be shuffled into other documents?"

Two days later, Chris requests the same document. Joe's learned his lesson, so he staples the pages together. Chris holds up the report by the staple, waving it in front of Joe. "I'm on my way to the printer with this," Chris says. "How will they be able to copy it if the three pages are bound together?"

In both situations outlining their conditions of satisfaction would have gotten Marcia and Chris exactly what they wanted sparing Joe their wrath. Joe has a certain responsibility to ask, but Chris is making the request, so Chris has to take responsibility for what he wants.

Crumbling Walls

A FEW YEARS ago, a contractor came to plaster, sand, and paint some interior portions of my house. I was out of town for a few days and so I didn't see the work until after I came home. I wasn't happy. The patches showed through the paint, leaving bumps and shadows all over the walls. When I called the office, a woman assured me that the contractor was competent and that he'd be back to fix things.

A few weeks passed and he didn't show, so I called another company. This time I was able to say, "Please be sure the walls are smooth and do whatever it takes to conceal the areas that were repaired. The areas are in my living room ceiling and in the corner of my bedroom." Now I knew what I didn't want, and I was able to articulate it. I was also able to be very specific about how I did want the problem areas to look when he was through, and detail what needed to be done. With these objectives in mind, he was able to respond and I ultimately got the job done the way I wanted it. (Incidentally, the first contractor called weeks after the job was done right and was angry that I had gotten someone else to complete his work.)

Promises

When one person issues a request, and the other person agrees to fulfill the request, a promise is made. Broken promises are always a source of anger and resentment, and they can usually be attributed to the fact that the promise was a higher priority for one party than it was for the other. A promise could begin with something as simple as, "Can you meet me at my house at 8 P.M. for dinner?" (request); when the person says "yes," the promise has been made. When he shows up, the promise has been fulfilled. In business, promises are made every day. A business offers a service and when that offer is accepted, a promise is initiated.

Problems arise when one party doesn't recognize the other's conditions of satisfaction, or doesn't respect them enough to fulfill the promise. The person issuing the request has to be clear: "This is important to me." "Can you get it here by the end of the week?" carries different weight than "If it isn't here by 3 P.M. on Friday, I will lose my job." The chances for promises to be broken decrease when the listener understands just how critical it is for her to come through. It also helps if she knows the consequences. Using specific language to seal a promise is critical. Phrases like "I agree to . . ." or "I will . . ." let the other party know the promise is secure. But using words like "I'll try . . ." or "I'll do my best to . . ." give the requester the hint that the promise isn't solid.

High-Voltage Vitamins

BEA WENT TO the health food store on Monday to order some vitamins that she needed right away. The saleswoman said that she would check on them and hopefully get them in on Wednesday. Bea returned to the store on Wednesday expecting to pick up five bottles, but only one had arrived. When she asked where the others were, the saleswoman explained that she was still checking on them and hadn't even ordered them yet.

Bea was furious. She screamed and yelled. The saleswoman was embarrassed. Her face turned red and she apologized profusely. Bea screamed some more. The saleswoman promised she would order them immediately and let Bea know exactly when they would be delivered.

Bea finally realized that her tirade wasn't going to bring the vitamins any faster. When she started to calm down, she also realized that she hadn't communicated clearly how crucial it was for her to have all the vitamins and to have them as soon as possible.

It is both the speaker's responsibility and the listener's responsibility to make sure they have reached an understanding. As the speaker, you must do whatever you can to make sure the other person gets the message. Just because you say it, doesn't mean it was heard. While Bea may have been clear about what she wanted, she hadn't been specific about when. All elements of a request have to be present in order for it to be effectively fulfilled.

Breaking the Promise

Do you scramble to fulfill a promise at all costs? What happens when you fail? You probably fear the reaction of the person you're letting down. You may even become defensive: "Well, you didn't give me enough time." You may make excuses: "My cat died." You may even direct your anger toward the person you made the promise to: "Why did you ask me to do that, anyway?"

We can't always live up to our promises. But we can revoke them responsibly. Own up to your mistake as soon as you see that you won't be able to fulfill the promise. The longer you wait, the worse it will be. Prepare for the person to be disappointed or angry, and allow him or her to experience that emotion.

Then, predict the consequences the person is going to face, and do what you can to alleviate them. An offer to make amends diminishes the impact of your not fulfilling your commitment: "I'm sorry I didn't get those reports done in time. I'll copy them myself and bring them to your meeting." Breaking a promise is not such a bad thing as long as you acknowledge it and fix your mistake. It's the unacknowledged blame and excuses that cause difficulty in communication. When your difficult people break promises, call them on it. "OK. So you won't have it ready by tomorrow. When will it be ready?" Don't let them off the hook.

Offers

Another way promises are formed are through offers. An offer is how we give respect to someone else's concerns, and suggest how we can take care of those concerns. Formal offers are made routinely in the workplace: "I offer myself to perform a service for you." "I offer you this salary in exchange for your service."

Be clear about what you're offering, and what the person considering the offer can expect. If I offer to give a full-day seminar, my client can expect me to arrive at 9 A.M., stay until 4 P.M., and give a talk about dealing with difficult people. He can't expect me to provide lunch. But if I'm not clear about my offer, he might think lunch is included. Both requests and offers need to be specific so that both parties are clear about how to produce success. When you make promises, always remember that the other person's interpretation of the promise's elements may be different from yours. If you are specifying a time, for instance, remember that 6 P.M. to you may be 6:15 or 6:30 to someone else. Check for other possible interpretations of the promise that may arise because of someone's personality or background.

Gaining Understanding Through Experience

Alter your expectations to accommodate what you know about someone's personality. If you realize that a person's behavior takes on a predictable pattern, you can anticipate that behavior and not let it bother you.

I have friend who, if she tells me to come over at 7:30 and I show up on her doorstep at 7:31, wants to know where I've been, and I'd better have a good excuse for being late. I have another friend who doesn't show up until 8:00 for 7:30 appointments.

Instead of upsetting the first friend, I always plan to be a few minutes early. And instead of being upset by the second friend, I expect her to be late. If I need her to arrive at 7:30, I tell her to be there at 7:00.

Would I be entitled to anger if she consistently showed up late, time after time, even though she promises to be on time? Yes, but that would cause a rift in an otherwise lovely friendship. I'd rather change my expectations, let go of the self-righteousness, and maintain a smooth course with a person I care for.

Declarations

Declarations are statements made in the present that change the future. When two people in a romantic relationship say "I love you" for the first time, it creates a new context for the relationship and also sets up implications for commitment.

When someone says, "I forgive you," it means that whatever happens in the future will not be influenced by past sins; the forgiver won't hold a grudge.

When a clergyman says, "I pronounce you man and wife," it significantly changes the life of two people.

Difficulties can arise when the appropriate declarations are absent. One of the most common complaints about difficult people is that they don't say "Good morning." They don't make any declarations of greeting. Those declarations and pleasantries say, "I recognize you as a human being." They validate you.

Other important declarations include "Thank you" (which conveys appreciation, gratitude and recognition) and "Welcome" (which says I'm glad you're here). Think about how these short phrases can make a difference in a person's day, and how they set the tone for the relationship that follows.

Often it's the declarations in our relationships that make or break them. Say "You are terrible" to someone and the direction of the relationship goes one way. Say "You are wonderful" and it goes another. What are the declarations your difficult person has made to influence his or her relationship with you? What declarations have you made? What happens when declarations aren't present? In most cases it's a great opportunity for assumption.

Complaints

When people don't get what they want, they end up complaining. But what is really happening when a complaint is issued? What are people really asking for?

Every complaint is a hidden request. How the complaint is handled is a bigger issue than what is wrong. The person complaining wants to be heard, and he wants the listener to respect him enough to take some kind of action.

Randi took her best friend to her favorite restaurant, a very popular eatery favored by critics and patrons for miles around. The atmosphere was elegant, the service was attentive, and the food lived up to its excellent reputation.

Midway through her chicken in cream sauce, Randi's companion bit down on a coiled peace of metal, scraping the inside of her cheek. Both of them were quite surprised, but they continued the meal.

At the end of the meal, they brought it to the attention of the manager. Not only did the manager offer her profuse apologies, but she gave them their dinner for free, and she also invited them back for another dinner on the house. She gave Randi's friend her card, and said the restaurant would pay her doctor or dental bills if she needed treatment.

What did Randi's friend hope to achieve by calling the foreign object to the manager's attention? She wanted an expression of concern, and assurance that she would be taken care of. Had the manager responded differently, Randi and her friend would have left with a very bad opinion of the place, and probably would have repeated the story of the metal and the mistreatment many times over. But the manager did everything she could to put things right, and to show that these customers were valuable to her. She saw the complaint as a request for some kind of action on the restaurant's part, and she obliged.

When someone complains, seminar leader Steven Gaff-
ney likes to ask, "What do you think we should do about
it?" This way the responsibility is on both parties to create
a solution. If the person tries to put it on you, bring it
back to the team effort by saying, "Let's brainstorm it,"
or, "Two heads are better than yours. Your input is valuable."

Things do go wrong, and nobody expects perfection.
But people do expect recognition when mistakes are made,
and expect someone to take responsibility for what went
awry (assuming it is truly their fault). We also expect ac-
knowledgment of the consequence to us, and some kind
of reparation made.

But what does making requests and promises do for us
at work and in the world? Why should we keep our commitments? As we examine this more closely, we see that
making effective requests, offers, and promises gets us
what many people crave: power.

Thought into Action

TRY TO PARAPHRASE or reiterate a conversation in which commitments are being made. Use gentle techniques like this: "I'll get off work at 3:00, so I'll be by to pick up that order around 4:00. Is that OK? Will you be at your desk at that time?" or "If I come to pick it up and you aren't here, will you leave it at the front desk with my name on it?" What are the consequences if they fail? Spell them out ahead of time.

ELEVEN

The Power of One

Vote for Me and I'll Set You Free!

One's ability to make requests and elicit promises from people is how one becomes more powerful.

Take the president of the United States. Most people would agree, regardless of their politics, that whoever holds that position is one of the most powerful people in the world. How does one get to be president? By making a lot of requests and getting a lot of promises in return. Some requests are big and involve a great deal of commitment: "Will you manage my campaign?" Others are smaller: "Will you vote for me?"

The candidate's ability to get people to say yes to his or her requests is directly related to his or her ability to get elected. People think of power as charisma or some other elusive, undefinable quality. But it really boils down to this: One who is capable of making requests and securing promises is powerful.

Power and Control

Power is the capacity for action. Powerful people get things done. There's a difference between being able to motivate and inspire people to get things done, and bullying people to get things done. Whether it is done negatively or positively, it is still power.

If you perceive that a co-worker is power hungry, or grasping for power, you may resent him. The opposite may be true as well. Your difficult person may think that you're vying for power—power over the situation, power within the workplace, and power over him. He may be right, or he may be interpreting your achievements, and the rewards they bring, as your deliberate pursuit of power.

When you try to seize control, you turn against the direction something is going. But control is an illusion. You can never really control someone else. What do you perceive to be the payoff of trying? What really happens? How do you feel when you think someone is trying to control you?

People who don't trust or accept their relationships are compelled to exert control. For example, young girls who don't have faith in their friends' loyalty will often try to control them by getting angry if they talk to other girls and threatening to pull out of a friendship over some minor violation. Grown men and women who feel insecure about themselves and doubt their partner's fidelity try to control that person by limiting his or her activities or expressing hostility.

If you give yourself power, and act powerfully with yourself, others will think of you as powerful. If we agree that your personality changes from relationship to relationship, then you can see that your level of power also changes. Is there a person to whom you attribute greater authority than you do to others? If so, you may be giving less authority to yourself in that person's presence. Are you aware of how your own perception of your power changes from person to person? Do you give your power away?

Who's on Top?

If you pair an aggressive man who needs to control with an aggressive woman who needs control, who gets the control? It becomes a constant battle, with each partner struggling to dominate. Most difficult relationships are about a fight for control.

If you need to control, and you're with someone with the same need, you're in trouble. Somebody is going to have to give up control, or else you have no place to go in the relationship. This is why letting go is so important for making progress.

People are afraid of giving up control. Examining the consequences and the benefits of relinquishing control and abandoning the fight for it may help. What you lose by letting go is the sparring and fighting. What you gain is cooperation, growth, and the chance to make things work. You may also lose face. You may have to swallow your pride and send your ego to the backseat. You may lose looking good and being right. But you will gain so much more.

When you give someone else control, you are actually in control, because you have made the conscious decision to do so. You are in control of who gets control. James Kouzes and Barry Posner, authors of *The Leadership Challenge,* say, "The more power you give away, the more power you have."

Some people confuse giving up control with becoming passive. Someone who feels the need to control may see this as a very black-and-white issue: "Either I am in control or I am controlled." But you can stop battling for control and still take care of yourself. One way to do that is to give up having to have something that isn't that important. Give up *something,* whether it's something you're negotiating, an assessment you have, or your attitude toward that person. The other person will see you pulling back and will probably respond in kind.

When we assume control of ourselves, and stop trying to control others, suddenly our effort to control becomes successful. We can't really change anyone except ourselves. Culturally, we are fighters. Our cultural assessment of working harder is better. We like to have a project to work on, a goal to achieve. Think of how Americans united against their enemies during the big wars. Making the effort as a team makes us feel good about ourselves, and included in something larger.

Sometimes our goal is to change someone else. We think if we just give it one more chance, just say the right thing, we can make it work. But that isn't always the answer. What are you fighting to get, or to keep? Is it worth it? What would happen if you just let go? Would it be more productive?

Kids vs. Grown-ups

The relationships between children and their guardians follow some of the most classic patterns of control, power, and struggle. Suppose a mother wants her kid to get dressed, and right now! Her child is frustrated by how little control he has in general, so he dawdles, fights, or rejects the clothes she's chosen.

This usually leads to a battle of wills, with the mother and the child each maneuvering to dominate. Their voices escalate, and the mother begins to use the weapons she has come by through age and position: She can threaten to punish or strike the child, take away favored toys, or physically force the child into the clothes.

"Winning" this struggle for control means the mother has overpowered the child. He remains frustrated and angry, and his feelings of powerlessness have been reinforced. While it may be true that he is dressed, the encounter has not done much for their relationship, and the struggle is bound to replay itself many times over.

Child development experts suggest offering children a choice. "Would you like to wear the green shirt or the red?" will get you out the door faster than "It's time to get dressed." Just like children, adults are more cooperative when they have a say in a situation. Can you do something to make your difficult person feel included in your efforts, instead of controlled by the way you want things done? Giving up some of your struggle for control may be as simple as asking your difficult person's opinion, offering her choices, and involving her in the process.

Control in the Workplace

Some organizations are built around a structure of control. They tell you when you will arrive and when you will leave, what you can wear, who you can talk to. Some of these guidelines are practical; for example, factory workers must wear protective clothing.

But if people aren't allowed to make some decisions and take some responsibility for themselves, they resent it. Employees who feel as though they're being treated like children tend to act childishly. Each person needs varying degrees of structure, and each person has a different level of tolerance for the rules and limitations imposed upon him or her in the workplace.

Perhaps the oppression your difficult person visits on you comes from a higher level, or stems from an interpretation (accurate or misguided) of company policy. Or

CLOSE TO HOME   JOHN McPHERSON

"Granted, the cast has to stay on for the next 37
weeks, but at least this way you can still
get around."

maybe he feels controlled by others, and is venting his
frustration by passing it along to you.

Power isn't necessarily defined by the position we hold,
but *by the way* we hold whatever position we have. Initially, people may respond to you, but when they find out
you don't walk your talk, you lose power in their eyes.
Power is defined as the capacity for action that is, action
aligned with our values and integrity. Mike Wallace once
interviewed Kofi Annan, the former secretary-general of

Clawing Up or Climbing Up?

LILI WENT TO work for a small, struggling company, one everyone knew was destined for greatness. Because the enterprise was so new, the managers couldn't afford to hire the most experienced professionals in the field. Instead, they gave jobs to energetic, sharp men and women recently out of college.

As the company grew, some people rose very quickly through the ranks. Lili thought those advancing the fastest were maneuvering for power, and she wondered why she wasn't being swept along with this tide of success. What she didn't realize was that the people advancing the fastest were the most talented, and the hardest working. She wasn't able to distinguish the difference between grabbing power and earning it.

the United Nations, on *60 Minutes* regarding the Iraqi crisis. He asked Mr. Annan, "Are you tough enough to negotiate with Saddam Hussein?" Mr. Annan's responded, "What is tough? We think of tough as yelling or pounding your feet, but tough is inner strength."

But how does this power live in our body? How do our bodies speak about us when our lips aren't moving? It's time to look at how what we don't say influences what we do.

Thought into Action

How do you give yourself power? Here are four things you can try:

On the physical level: First, put your hand on your belly button. This is your power center. Press gently, and focus on that area. Imagine there's a connection, a circuit between your center and the ground. Feel your feet being pulled by the earth. Use touching your center as a lightning rod to draw in the stabilizing power of the earth.

On the emotional level: Second, remember how it felt to be powerful. Recall a situation in which you felt strong and in control. How did you speak? What was your body doing? Assume the elements of that powerful moment, and transfer them to this new situation. If you can't remember a time for yourself, think of someone you consider powerful. How does that person speak? Hold his or her body? Who can you emulate?

On the Mental Level: Third, think of the payoff. Concentrate on what you'll gain from maintaining power. How will you feel? What will the rewards be? Who can you talk to about how they got to be in a position of power? List the elements that make them powerful. How can you incorporate these qualities into your behavior?

Back to the Physical Level: Last, bring the power into your body. Summon all of the characteristics of a powerful person, and incorporate them into your actions. How does that person walk? Talk? Hold his or her body? Dress? How can you bring all these ingredients into the mix of you and express it your own way?

Remember these elements as you are about to face a difficult person. Bringing power into your body will allow you to deal with difficult circumstances with more dignity and confidence. Even if these behaviors don't feel natural yet, do them anyway. Fake it till you make it. Act powerful and you'll be powerful.

· T W E L V E ·

Your Body Is Speaking— Are You Listening?

TV Guy

A television reporter stopped Christina on the street and asked her to appear on camera. Christina answered a few questions, and since the piece wouldn't be aired locally, requested a copy of the tape. The reporter said she should call the office in a few days to make the arrangements. When Christina called, an intern explained that the reporter wasn't there anymore and the network would not issue a copy of the tape.

Christina was confused. The reporter had been functioning as a representative of this company, and the company now possessed a piece of tape with her face, voice, and name on it. She felt she was entitled to see how she had been represented. "What can I do at this point?" she asked the intern. "There is nothing you can do," the intern insisted. Christina didn't accept this as the end of the discussion. "If I had my lawyer request it, could I get a copy?" Christina asked.

The intern said politely, "My boss can explain the policy."

A man (his boss) picked up the phone. Christina calmly explained again that she was trying to get a copy of a tape she had appeared in. Rather than refusing to send it, he told her he would take care of it.

She thanked him and hung up. A few minutes later, the boss man called back. "You neglected to tell me that you threatened my intern," he screamed.

"I didn't threaten him, I merely asked a question," she explained, shocked that this person was yelling at her.

"We don't like threats. Your request is denied." And he slammed down the phone.

Christina spent the next few hours feeling horrible. At first she thought, "What a jerk." Then she got angry, and thought, "Who the hell does he think he is?" Then she started to wonder, "Did I do something wrong?"

His tirade made her aware that she'd said something she shouldn't have. His angry words were like a pin pricking at something deep inside that she felt bad about. Christina's stomach knotted and her head pounded. She was much more stressed by this exchange than she expected to be. She found it especially uncomfortable to be the target of a stranger's anger. In her mind, anger was an intimate emotion, one best expressed within the bounds of a safe, nurturing relationship.

She also felt irritable. When her two-year-old son approached her with a stack of building blocks, her immediate reaction was to hold up her hand with her palm facing him. By giving him this stop sign, she could literally keep him at arm's length. By pushing him away, she could continue to wallow in the anger and the anguish.

Then she decided to change what she did with her body, and change her words. As she extended her arm, instead of turning her palm toward him, she deliberately and almost forcibly turned it upward, accepting the blocks into her hand. Instead of saying, "Mommy doesn't feel like playing right now," she said, "What color should we put on the bottom?" It felt strange at first. In fact, she heard her voice coming from a distance, as if it were someone else's.

But the simple act of rotating her hand upward released the tension in her stomach. And the decision to change her words, even though she struggled to do it, stopped the pounding in her head. Soon she had gained control of her emotions, and the anger evaporated like a cloud of steam.

Not only did she relieve herself of a cycle of negativity, but she also avoided passing on the anger to her child. What if she'd made him feel unwanted and resentful? He might have hit someone on the playground. And that child might have been so cranky that he'd ruin his own mother's day. And so on and so on. Even though she never got the tape, she learned a lesson about how such a small incident could have affected so many.

*   *   *

The Weber-Fechner law, a psychological principle, asserts that our ability to detect change in a stimulus varies in direct proportion to the intensity of the stimulus. In other words, what we perceive is based on the context we see it in. Put an ant on an elephant and you hardly notice it, but put the ant on a leaf and it becomes more visible. Small changes can have big impact. Like Christina did, try making a small change in yourself, and see how you experience it in a larger way.

I Brake for Difficult People

There are two basic steps to retraining our thoughts about—and our bodily reactions to—difficult people. First, we have to become aware of the situation, of our role in the situation, and of the power we have to act differently to affect the outcome of the situation. Second, we have to retrain our response.

Remember the exercise in the beginning of the book, where I told you to entwine your fingers to see which thumb ended up on top? Do it again, but this time put the opposite thumb on top. Notice how odd it feels. If you force yourself to put the nondominant thumb on top, over and over, it will begin to feel natural. After a while you may forget which one started out as the dominant one.

When we learn new habits and new ways of behaving, it feels weird at first, whether it's our thumb or destructive habits. To take on a new habit involves stepping outside our comfort zone and imagining the possibilities. What does an anger habit cost? What are the benefits to reversing that habit? What are the risks of continuing with it?

Researchers at the Institute of Heartmath, a nonprofit think tank in California, have produced some interesting data. They discovered that the memory of an angry or frustrating experience depletes the body's supply of IgA, an immune system antibody that fights colds and flu. Merely recalling that situation for five minutes is enough to drain IgA to levels so low it takes six hours to restore.

By contrast, this same study showed that one five-minute period spent remembering a time of care and compassion created an immediate rise in IgA, bolstering the immune system and causing those levels to continue increasing for the next six hours. Therefore, care and compassion don't just feel good—they're healthful!

One way to break the negative habitual response pattern is the ABS braking system for internal stress. Learn the following mnemonic. It will give you something easy enough to remember during a moment of crisis. Use it to preempt your habitual response cycle. This simple model incorporates an observation, the power of breathing, and the power of the mind. It's the combination and simplicity of the three that makes the technique powerful. In a car, the ABS braking system keeps your brakes from locking. Here it keeps us from being locked into unproductive old habits.

A—Awareness

Think of this as witnessing. Observe your reaction objectively. Being aware of your state provides the first clue for shifting it. It's your baseline or benchmark. It's as easy as saying to yourself, "I'm stressed," or "Look at how I'm reacting." Notice what sparked your response, then notice the response.

B—Breathing

We know that the physiological link between our mental and physical stressors and one of the best ways to release tension is through breathing. The focus of this breath is a bit different. Imagine yourself breathing through your heart, allowing the air to travel deep into your body and out again.

The split second you spend thinking about this inhalation allows you to gain control, take a step back, and be neutral. It also stops your muscles from clenching, provides the brain with extra oxygen, and slows down the automatic responses you might otherwise fall into.

S—Shift

When were you happy? At the beach? In front of a fire? On a sunny Sunday in the park? Remember a scenario that makes you completely serene. Practice calling it up until it comes to your mind with photographic clarity.

This shifts your emotional state. Flash back to that pleasant time, a time that brings you contentment or joy. Be ready to call it up quickly. The memory should make you feel good enough for the moment it takes to do something different than your normal pattern would dictate.

If this doesn't work, move into the future. Will you be this upset tomorrow? Next month? Shift into the larger perspective. How does this fit into the big picture? How much does it really matter?

ABS into Action

CLOSE YOUR EYES. Remember a time when you were frustrated or angry. Picture the scene in your mind. Examine the feelings the memory produces in your body. How intense are these sensations? Are they mild, or unbearable? Describe the feelings: "I'm aware of stress." "My stomach is knotted." "My jaw feels tight."

Now think of your heart as the facilitator of breathing. As you draw breath, its warmth flows into the area experiencing the effects of the stress. Focusing on the heart brings about changes in all the body's systems. They align, providing clarity and inner balance.

As you exhale, imagine you're expelling the stress. Imagine each molecule of carbon dioxide carrying a tiny bit of it away. Allow your heart to breathe for you. Think of it as working in unison with your lungs.

Then shift. Replace the troubling scenario with a relaxing one. Shifting your thoughts to another time and place will activate a reversal of the physical discomfort. Think about a time in the past when you were content. Or imagine looking back ten years from now at this situation that causes you aggravation. What do you see, feel, hear? Examine the sensations of peace and calm just as you did the sensations of stress. Remember the areas that experience the relaxation.

Applying the Brakes

A friend who owns a speakers bureau recently called, upset because the speaker he had booked for an engagement coming up the following month had called to cancel. Apparently a friend of his had seen the speaker didn't like what he saw, and told my friend, who in turn had encouraged the speaker to change some of his speech. The speaker was furious at the suggestion and canceled the engagement. My friend was prepared to act from his emotion, call the speaker back, and tell him where to go. He called me instead.

After we hashed it out for a few minutes, I pointed his emotional state out to him. He agreed. No news here. Then I asked him to take a few deep breaths. As he did, his state began to change. His breathing began to shift his perspective. Then I told him to imagine that it was a year from now, that the incident was over, however it turned out, and he was sitting in the exact same chair in his house. "How do you feel a year from now?" I asked him. "Fine. Unaffected," he replied. In the span of a few minutes he had shifted completely out of his irate emotional state and was prepared to deal with the situation. He called the speaker back and told him that it was fine if he chose not to come, but that he was worried about how it might look not only for the organization that was bringing the speaker in, but for the speaker as well. He saw that both reputations were at stake. He also explained that his only interest was in making the presentation the best that it could be, and that his suggestions for the changes in the program were not mandatory, but simply ideas for an even better program. The speaker thought about their conversation overnight. In the morning he called back and agreed to the program. It was a huge success.

ABS doesn't solve your problem. It puts you into a mood where *you* can.

Bestselling author Deepak Chopra said: "By becoming a conscious choice-maker, you begin to generate actions that are evolutionary for you and for those that are around you." Apply the ABS, and change your habits, your choices, and your future.

Thought into Action

REMEMBER AN EXCHANGE with your difficult person. What were your negative reactions? Where did you feel it in your body? How long did it last? Recognize what your language and body are like when you are experiencing different emotions. Do your facial muscles tighten when you're happy and relaxed? Do you fidget when you're calm? If you can incorporate control over language and body into difficult situations, you will have less trouble controlling your emotions. Anger, anxiety, and tension are the real reasons difficult people affect us.

Replace something negative you said with a positive word or positive action. Then replay the situation, substituting positive for negative. How might the result differ? Did you notice a difference in your body? Candace Pert, a former NIMH researcher, tells us that we experience molecules of emotion in every aspect of our being. Are you aware of where you are experiencing yours? Once you've identified these physical triggers, you can see them as waves passing through and not feel as obligated to respond to them. You can see them as one perspective and not the only reality. Then you have more options for response.

What would it have meant to rise above in that situation? Could you have diffused the problem? Could you have come away feeling better about yourself? Be prepared for the scene to replay itself; with difficult people, it usually does. Change one small thing about your body as Christina did: a hand, posture, facial expression, and so on. And notice whether your emotions shift.

Here are four steps you can take: (1) Tune in and become aware of the body element and where you are experiencing emotions. (2) Wait: Let the emotion pass. (3) Open your body position including hands, eyes, arms, and so on. (4) React from your center instead of your emotion. By changing your posture, body language, thinking, and speaking, the emotion will come down, and the intensity will thin itself out.

THIRTEEN

Mirror, Mirror in Your Face

If you look closely at any image the world presents to you, more and more of your own self will start peering back.

—*Deepak Chopra*, The Way of the Wizard

A few years ago I went to buy a new car. I test-drove one, but it wasn't quite what I wanted. The salesman noticed my disappointment and suggested another. I had never heard of or seen this model, but I agreed to give it a spin. After two minutes in the car I knew it was the one for me. I bought it the next day. When I drove the car off the lot, I was amazed to find that everyone else had the same car. All of a sudden they were everywhere. How could this be? Did all these other drivers just buy this car, or had I just not noticed? And why was I noticing now?

In psychology, this concept is known as *scotoma*. It exists on the physical level. Projection is the same principle applied to the arena of personality. Projection is reflection. Why is it that some people drive you crazy and others don't affect you at all? Are others affected by the same people that drive you crazy? What is it about them that digs in, rearranges your emotional state, and makes you so attuned to the negativity?

When I was in college I suffered from anorexia, a disease of perception. When an anorexic looks in the mirror she sees fat, no matter how skinny she is. At the time I weighed seventy-five pounds—nearly thirty pounds less than my current weight—and I stand only 5'3" tall. People told me I was skinny, but through my distorted internal mirror, all I saw was fat. My mother saw the danger and threatened to put me in a hospital and feed me through a tube.

During this time, I went on a trip with a bunch of other college students. One of my traveling companions had just been released from a hospital where she had been treated for anorexia, and she described her ordeal in detail. She spoke of endless needle sticks, of being force-fed, of having no say in her own care, and of being treated like an animal. She painted such an ominous, painful picture that I was instantly sobered. I resolved to change my eating habits.

It's amazing how we struggle to move toward pleasure and away from pain. At this point eating was looking more enjoyable. The consequences of not eating were more than I could bear.

Whenever I met someone during that period I evaluated

his or her weight. I spoke about people in terms of how fat or skinny they were. If someone were to say "Did you meet Susan?" I would respond, "You mean the skinny girl in physics?" Because I was so focused on that issue, the world appeared to be similarly focused. If you didn't know anything about projection, you might look at the person about whom I was speaking, rather than at me. But projection is always much more about whose lips are flapping than what they're flapping about. I continued to judge others, as we all do, based on what was important to me at the time, and what I was insecure about.

Gradually I figured out that I had a problem not only with my weight, but also with my view of the world. Emotionally, I had hit rock bottom. I started taking personal-development seminars and tried to look at myself in the context of others. Consequently, as I began to discover more of the goodness inside me, I began to see it in others as well. My good feelings about myself began to show up in the faces of others. Had they changed? Probably not.

I became less concerned about how I looked and less concerned about others' looks in the process. As I was discovering the light in me, others began to shine. I was no longer the victim of my own subconscious. When I saw what I was doing, my world changed.

Reflections in the Mirror

How are you being blinded by your own thoughts? Are you awake enough in the present to see what's in front of you? What you look for and what you see is a reflection of you. If you're so busy looking for people's difficultness, you'll never get to see the wonderful parts.

Who is the person looking out? How can you take off your blinders and discover what you don't know about yourself? How can the outside world show you what you need to work on? What can your difficult people teach you? Try the following self-assessment.

Do You See What I See?

1. List three characteristics your difficult people have that you don't like:

   _____   _____   _____

2. List three characteristics your parents have that you don't like:

   _____   _____   _____

3. List three characteristics you have that you don't like:

   _____   _____   _____

Are there any parallels among these three lists? Any overlap? Are you finding opposite characteristics? Are your difficult people overly rude, while you are overly nice?

After doing this exercise in one of my seminars, a man said his difficult person was angry and that he was a quiet, calm man. He claimed he never got angry. I've never met anyone who doesn't get angry. It's a human emotion, as basic as love, sadness, fear, and joy. He explained that when he was young he was taught that expressions of anger are impolite and rude.

This man *does* become angry; he just doesn't express it. When he feels it, he suppresses it until it passes. It also turns out that his health isn't very good. When I heard that, the pieces fell into place. He believes that it is inappropriate for him to express anger; therefore, when he sees someone else doing it, it drives him nuts. If he can't express his anger, why should someone else be allowed to? When we deny ourselves, we feel self-righteous and a little resentful. When we see others indulging in what we have denied ourselves, we often lash out, criticize, fill with disdain, and secretly envy them. What we rarely do is own our envy.

This tendency is an expression of painful parts of ourselves that lurk in our internal shadows, the parts that live in us and infect us, but that we are unwilling to expose. We have to learn to accept the shadowy, dark parts of our personalities in order to accept ourselves completely and, in turn, to be accepted by others. This can be a difficult process, but awareness of our tendencies opens the door to resolution of our problems.

Now that you have an understanding of projection, what do you do with it? When someone or something bothers you, you can ask, "What is this revealing about me? What is this showing me that up until now I have ignored? Why does it (this person's behavior) bother me so much?" Bill Campbell, the former mayor of Atlanta, puts it succinctly when he says, "In dealing with difficult people, I try to remember that everything that irritates us about others can lead us to an understanding of ourselves."

In Your Own Image

When faced with a difficult person, start by understanding yourself. Take the difficult person out of the equation and look inside. Chances are you'll find a dirty secret lurking within: That person reflects back to you a part of yourself you don't like.

It's not easy to accept, but often the reason someone really bothers us, rubs like new shoes on a callus, is that we see in him or her an undesirable element of our own personality, magnified.

Why do you react the way you do to a difficult person? Do you want to change these patterns, gain awareness, reflect on your own personality, and explore solutions?

Honesty Night

A FEW YEARS ago my women's group had an "honesty night." The other nights weren't "dishonesty nights," but this night we agreed to be extremely frank about the good and bad things we saw in each other. This night was set aside as an opportunity to get to know each other on a deeper level and discuss barriers to our relationships with one another. We took turns going to each person and when it was my turn, one of the women said, "I hate your guts. The sight of you makes me nauseous. I'm anxious all day long at the thought of seeing your face."

That day I happened to have been in a pretty good mood, and I felt strong and content inside. Instead of being upset or taking it personally, I reacted by asking, "What is it you hate about me so much? Remember, this is honesty night." At the time I was the team leader of the group, and I ran it much as I would a seminar, deciding the agenda and creating a program for each meeting.

She replied, "You tell us what we're going to do rather than ask us what we want. You're a show-off, an actress, and a fake."

I said, "Okay, what is it about me that reminds you of you? What of yourself do you see reflected in me?"

She became very quiet for a moment. "Well, there are times when I *am* a show-off, and a bit of an actress," she admitted, "and I want to be in charge!" I asked her what she would do if she had that chance. She shared her vision for the group and told me what was important to her. We went over a few more of the things that bothered her, and then I asked, "Now how do you feel about me?" "Better," she said.

That moment was a turning point in our relationship. The power that those thoughts had had over her was gone. Her resentment had been vented and had evaporated in the wind. Although we never became good friends, she still keeps up with me through a mutual acquaintance. Once she took the spotlight off me and shone it on herself, she began to see that there was nothing "out there" to hate.

Haven't We Met?

Sometimes you can be the victim of someone else's bad relationship. When difficult people play out their problems from other situations with you, it's known as transference.

Susan's boss, Jim, reminds her of her father, with whom she had a difficult relationship. Whenever she is around Jim, her early frustrations surface, and she reverts to the actions and responses of her childhood. So her boss assumes the role of her father, and she assumes the role of the young Susan.

Because people relate to you positionally first and personally second, they act according to the context they see you in. As people work together and get to know each other, that can change. Initially, however, we size people up, and the information we get from our evaluation is the foundation for how we are around them. The feelings we have toward people in certain positions define our actions and the perspective from which we speak to them. Some people will instantly speak to lawyers with respect, others react with complete disdain, and others still will trot out their best anti-lawyer jokes. It all depends on what opinion the speaker holds about members of the legal profession.

Wouldn't you address your best friend differently than you address your boss or a client? What if someone applies her prejudices to your position? You can ask directly, "Do I remind you of someone else in your life?" She may even recognize the similarity herself, and sometimes just identifying that this is an issue is enough to help her see past it. In most cases the connection between you and someone else that measured significantly on her relationship meter won't be clear.

If you discover that you remind your difficult person of someone else, take these three steps. First, find out what you're doing that is just like his mother, brother, or ex-lover. Ask someone who knows his family, or even perhaps ask the person himself. Second, do something different. Let him know that you aren't that person, and eliminate or attempt to change those actions that may remind him of this person. Perhaps it is not what you're doing, but rather how you're doing it.

Third, watch the dynamic between the two of you. If he rebels like a child when you give him an assignment, maybe you're acting like a parent. Firmly maintain the demeanor of an adult interacting with an adult, even when he pushes you into the role of parent. That's the place he feels comfortable, so it's in his best interest to lure you there. You can break the cycle by refusing to go. Watch people who have a good relationship with this person. What are they doing that you aren't?

Acting differently may be enough to jostle him out of those old habits. Try an unexpected or out-of-character remark and watch how he reacts. If it's common for you to engage in a cycle of blame, just sit back and say, "You're right. I'm sorry. I'll do my best not to let it happen again." It might be tough to put your ego on hold, but if you can make that change in yourself, you can start the wheels of change turning in him as well.

Now that you understand the mechanics behind why people act differently, let's look at your level of involvement. With some people, you really want to put an effort into the relationship; with others, you don't want to deal with the person. How can you evaluate what's at stake? How do you know when to hang on and when to let go?

FOURTEEN

Know When to Hold 'Em, Know When to Fold 'Em

What's at Stake?

Evaluate your problems in perspective. You handle the people you encounter casually in a different way from those you cannot avoid, or don't want to avoid.

Does your dry cleaner repeatedly fail to have your shirts ready by 5 P.M. on Tuesday? If you live in a big enough town, you can just go to another store. If you live on a military base and can't get your uniforms cleaned anywhere else, the stakes ratchet up a notch, and you may have to work on a solution.

Once you're married you can't change your mother-in-law. You have to deal with your kids' teachers, even if you'd prefer not to. And although you may be able to leave a job when you don't get along with co-workers, what will that do to your finances and to your career? In

CLOSE TO HOME   JOHN McPHERSON

"Go!"

these cases, the stakes are quite high. Leaving is always an option, but at what cost? Here is a situation where the individuals parted, but what was at stake wasn't money.

The Customer Is Always Right

Sally owns a commercial design and furnishing company. Her relationship with one particular client, Thomas, was fraught with problems. It came to a head when Thomas, with whom she had done business many times, wrote her a letter refusing to pay the $150 balance due on his purchases. He recounted all the issues that had troubled him, and declared he would never work with her again or refer her to anyone else. This guy was angry.

What's at stake here? He'd already paid thousands of dollars, so the money that was left was insignificant. But her reputation was in shambles. His poor opinion of her could spread and ultimately affect her business, especially since this client was an influential community leader.

What Sally had to lose was her good name. How could she remedy this? Maybe she couldn't satisfy this person to the point that he'd change his mind and work with her again, but she had to reverse his sentiment enough to keep him from bad-mouthing her to everyone he knew.

Unsure of how to handle the situation, Sally asked me for professional advice. I pointed out that she was stuck at "who's right or wrong" (I reminded her of all the times we've eaten in restaurants and how she expects managers/owners to take responsibility for food that isn't up to her standards). I suggested that she write Thomas a letter apologizing for the things that had gone wrong and for causing him so much frustration. She did, and also offered to make a donation to a charity equal to his balance, in his name. While this gesture didn't turn him into a loyal customer, it softened his anger and ended their relationship on a better note. When he received the letter, Thomas called Sally and thanked her for seeing his point of view. In the end she salvaged her reputation, which was her major concern, and both ultimately got what they wanted.

In interactions like this, one of the major elements that leads to a breakdown in communication is trust. With it, relationships flourish. When trust erodes, the relationship is doomed. What exactly is this thing we call trust and how do we create, keep, and deepen it with those we do business with, love, and simply interact with in life?

Trust

What is trust? There are three elements that lead us to trust someone. First, a person has to speak and carry himself in a way that makes him appear sincere. If he looks you directly in the eye and says, "I will meet you at 2:00 with the report," he appears sincere. If he shuffles his feet, looks away, and mumbles, "Well, uh, I'll try to get out of my other appointment and do what I can to meet you in the afternoon, but I'm not sure," you won't be so quick to believe him.

Second is reliability. If someone tells you she's going to do something, but she has failed to deliver on her commitments in the past, you probably won't trust her to be reliable. Reliability is often about showing up, about being somewhere when you say you will be. Almost every family has a member who is consistently late to gatherings or often won't show at all. What is your assessment of that person? Would you trust him or her to baby-sit?

Third is capability. Does the person have the experience, background, or talent to deliver on his promise? If you have a broken arm and I feel really bad for you and want to help you fix it, I may show up and express my deep concern for you. But since I'm not a doctor, you probably don't want me to set it for you. In this domain, you wouldn't trust that I can do the job. This is why we value experience in different arenas. It demonstrates capability so that we can trust that a job will get done.

An editor was interviewing writers to consult on a book. She tried to assess how much she trusted each applicant by these three indicators. She was able to get the most concrete information about the last: "Is this a capable writer? Does she have the talent, skill, and experience to do the job?" Reading her writing samples and looking at how she had performed in previous positions provided that information.

The sincerity part was not so obvious. Through conversations with the writers she tried to gauge how sincere they were about wanting the job. Somehow she had to measure, even by gut instinct, if they would be reliable. She decided to have lunch and evaluate each person. She looked to see whether they showed on time, judged how they presented themselves, and assessed their level of enthusiasm as they spoke about the project. She noticed whether they spoke more about the project or about themselves. It worked. She was able to pick the perfect person for the job and it proved successful.

At a certain point, you have to take a leap of faith. I will expect a person to keep an appointment with me, and if he doesn't show, he betrays my trust. I might be inclined to understand if he had an emergency, but the next time I'm going to be watching the clock very closely.

Repeated failures to honor commitments erode trust,

and once that happens, it is very hard to restore it. Passive people in particular tend to make promises that aren't realistic or practical, and end up being unable to keep them.

Sincerity would seem like a hard thing to judge, but we really do read people's body language all the time. Everyone has intuition, or a "gut feeling," but sometimes we ignore that little voice and end up regretting it. Perhaps intuition is a sixth sense, something metaphysical and hard to explain. But it could be our subconscious registering a shifting eye, a nervous twitch, or some other posture inconsistent with what the speaker is saying. We could be noticing incongruities without realizing we notice them. Something is out of kilter enough for us to mistrust.

Most people trust others until they have a reason not to. Some automatically distrust until others have "proven" themselves. The latter tend to cause difficulties, but their mistrust stems from a past rift that laid a foundation of paranoia. They think people are inherently bad. Learn not to take it personally. When someone doesn't trust you for any particular reason, chances are it's more about his or her deep-rooted issue with trust than anything you've said or done.

Your belief structure shows up in the world around you. Difficult people who think the world is bad and that people are going to disappoint them will find proof to support that theory. They're almost pleased when you let them down; then they can say, "See, I knew you couldn't be trusted." They're afraid of looking foolish, of people thinking they'd been duped or conned. If they expect you to fail, and you do, they can boast about their acute intuition.

A colleague and I were working on a project together. I knew that trust was an issue for him, so I did everything in my power to let him know that I was with him 100 percent: I showed up for meetings early, called to inquire about the project before he called me, and spent extra time researching material. Somehow through all of this I felt that he still wasn't convinced. He looked at me suspiciously at times, checked up to see if I was doing the work on time, and focused on the money aspects of the job. I could tell there was something he wasn't trusting, but I knew if I asked him he would deny it. I didn't know how to resolve his concern without addressing it. Then one night the company we were consulting for had a party. It was a celebration of their success over the last year, and I knew my colleague would be there and in good spirits. So I took the opportunity to write him a note and handed it to him at the party to bolster his festive mood. In the note, I thanked him for giving me what I knew he valued: trust. I thanked him for helping me with the client, for the support that he had given me, and for endowing me with his trust, which was so crucial to our success there. His eyes lit up when he read the note. It was as if I had seen into him; I understood him. From that moment on, the relationship changed. He tore down the wall of mistrust and I felt an ease coming from him that I'd never experienced before. In all our dealings since then, I have felt a degree of trust present that has allowed us to surge ahead in our communication with each other and for the company.

If you thank people for what you value, it causes them to unconsciously (or consciously) give it to you.

FIFTEEN

Uncommon Solutions to Common Problems

As you have been reading, you may have identified questions or scenarios that you haven't found answers to. Here are some real-life examples of people in my seminars that may help to address some of your real-life issues.

Problem: *In any given situation, your difficult person sparks that sudden surge of anger.*

Solution: There are five steps you can take to stem the tide.

1. **Count down.** When anger hits, allow it to move through your body like a speeding train barreling along a track. The flush you feel will only last about thirty seconds. Wait. This is the time when you have the least control, and when you might say something you'll regret later. Count to ten or tell yourself, "This will

pass." By the end of the countdown, you'll be able to regain your composure and act more rationally.

2. **Talk, talk, talk.** Confide in someone you trust. Say, "I hate to dump this on you, but I really need to vent." Then do it. Yell, cry, fume. Let her know how upset you are. Use her as a sounding board. Solicit her opinion. Try to find the real issue between you and your difficult person. A third party may have a perspective you lack. She may even turn out to be an ally. If nothing else, she can be a safety valve for your steam, and you can deal with your difficult person on a more intellectual (and less emotional) level.

3. **Move it out.** Do something physical. Go for a walk or swim. Get a tennis racquet and hit something (but not someone). Imagine yourself telling the person about your anger. In your head, scream, rant, and rave as you transfer your anger to a pillow, a ball, or a book. Pretend to tell him how this has affected you, or how unfair he's been. Movement can help your body rid itself of some of the tension anger causes. The less you feel your anger physically, the less intense the emotion will be.

4. **Write it out.** If you are still feeling upset, write it down. Doing a "data dump" will get it out of your head and body and onto paper. When you are calm, write down what you can learn from that person. Will you come out stronger? More aware? Less vulnerable?

5. **Carefrontation.** Now that you have short-circuited the anger, you can deal with the person if you choose. You've thought about the reasons you were upset, then released some of the upset. Now you can approach the situation rationally. Tell him how you feel and how his actions affected you. Speak about what you learned or are learning. Make it about you. You want him to listen and not get defensive. If he interrupts, ask him to "just listen" and then it will be his turn. Tell him you need to make your feelings known.

Be sure you know what you hope to gain from this discussion, and communicate that to him. Do you want to voice your concerns, or do you want him to do something differently? Say, "I'm telling you this because . . . ," so he knows what your expectations are. Make a request: "In the future, I would like you to . . ." By this time your anger should be diffused and it will be easier to have a meaningful conversation.

By following these steps, your expression of anger will be more cleansing for you, and more purposeful, direct, concrete, and productive for everyone involved. According to Tim Connor, certified speaking professional and author, anger can even offer benefits. He says it can be an excellent way to eliminate stress, get hidden agendas out in the open, and vent feelings of discouragement, pain, grief, or frustration. Suppressed negative feelings or anger can affect a person's emotional and physical well-being in the short term and over the long hall.

Problem: *A man called me in search of some guidance. He'd been blowing up at his wife, making sarcastic remarks, and feeling easily irritated. He asked me what he could do with all his hostility.*

Solution: Rather than speak the sarcasm, speak the frustration.

I told him that instead of saying something sarcastic, he should say, "I feel as if I want to say something sarcastic," or "My instinct right now is to say something sarcastic." Instead of exploding, say, "I am so angry I could just explode." Expressing the desire to act that way will stop you from acting that way, and will open the door to dialogue, rather than put you on either side of a field playing offense and defense. If he feels he needs to act something out, then doing something physical, like hitting a tennis racquet against a pillow or working out, will be just as effective. As Cheri Huber and Melinda Guyol say in *Time-Out for Parents*, "Having feelings and acting on them are two very different things, and it is crucial to understand the difference."

Problem: *Jane asks Joan to complete a project, but Joan's finished product reflects her own vision of the job instead of what Jane wanted.*

Solution: Get on the same page from the beginning.

Jane should have given Joan a summary or project analysis, and explained where the job was headed. Joan may not have understood where this particular task fit into a bigger picture, or she may not have realized that it had to be done a certain way to be consistent with other tasks of which she was unaware. Jane could also have had milestone checks with Joan throughout the project, to make sure she was on the right track. This would have helped Joan avoid wasting her time and feeling resentful.

Since it isn't too late, Jane could still try to incorporate some of Joan's ideas while maintaining the integrity of the final product, or she could find another job where Joan's vision would be more appropriately implemented. They can sit down and discuss where the breakdown in communication occurred and use it as an opportunity to create new language and distinctions between them for the future projects.

Problem: *Craig, Jim, and Mindy work in a shop with Allen. He's explosive, argumentative, and unreasonable. He rejects authority, routinely interrupts meetings, and changes his position just to be contrary. He has emotional and dependency problems that follow him to work.*

Outbursts aside, they like Allen. He does good work, and they consider him a friend. They want to see his difficult behavior end, but they still want to maintain their relationship with him.

Solution: The problem is that their relationship keeps them from setting boundaries. They haven't established rules or standards for conduct. They don't want to say anything hurtful or report him.

Unfortunately, Allen is being rewarded for his unpredictable emotional outbursts. Somebody in a position of authority needs to speak to him, outline how he is expected to behave at work, and what the consequences will be if he doesn't meet those expectations.

Another option is for the team to set standards for what will and won't be tolerated at work. He should have a role in establishing the rules, and when he breaks them, he needs to be punished. His co-workers need to make it clear to him that their friendship cannot insulate him from the repercussions brought on by his own destructive behavior.

Problem: *Someone you work with or know is always complaining about having no solutions to her problems. She always sees things from a negative perspective. She blames her incompetence on her limitations. "I don't have the resources. I don't have the time. My budget is too small."*

Solution: Ask her, "What resources *are* available to help you with this concern? Who can you talk to? How can you deal with this?" Whatever her complaint, point out that being limited is an opportunity for creativity, flexibility, and ingenuity. Whatever the problem, there's always a solution if you look hard enough. And the problem is always there for a reason; perhaps understanding the reason will provide the solution.

The *Washington Post* once carried a story about a political prisoner in a South American jail. He'd been kept in complete darkness in solitary confinement for years.

With nothing to do, and no sensory input, he feared that his sanity hung in the balance.

He pulled a button from his torn shirt. He twirled in circles, then threw the button across his cell. Then he combed the floor of the cell, one inch at a time, until he found his treasure, sometimes days later. Once he found it, he repeated the game to keep his mind alive, absorb himself in the new moment, and re-create his world. If the problem exists, then so does the solution. Asking is the necessary step to finding.

Problem: *For nearly thirty years, a librarian made life a living nightmare for her colleagues. She snooped in their offices, spied on them through the stacks, and arbitrarily denied vacation requests. She tried to control others, insulted and abused them, and never took responsibility for her own mistakes.*

Solution: When this happened to employees of a library in the Midwest they moved into action. Three employees brought their grievance against the librarian to an authority who launched an investigation. Before long, the librarian was "retired."

Problem: *In another library, a homeless man often came in and caused havoc. He would shout, talk to himself, and disturb the other patrons. When the librarian asked him to leave, he'd refuse. His odor was overwhelming, and despite the librarian's attempts to get him help, the social services agencies in the town hadn't intervened.*

Solution: Enlist the help of an authority. Some difficult people may respond only to security guards or police officers, and you must call them to your aid if your safety or the safety of others is at risk.

Some people are mentally ill or downright weird. Remember, being rational with someone who is irrational is pointless. Find someone who is trained to handle these extreme situations, especially when you're being threatened or intimidated.

Problem: *Your boss is intimidating. He yells, threatens, and insults you. He overwhelms you and strips you of your self-esteem.*

Solution: Give him the message that it isn't OK to talk to you this way, using reward and punishment. When he speaks kindly, respond immediately and thank him for making his request in that way. When he speaks inconsiderately, let him know that it's hard for you to fulfill his request. Just because he pays your salary doesn't mean that he has permission to abuse you. He will abide by the standards you set, if he wants you to continue working for him.

Parting Thoughts

John Hagemann, professor and librarian at the University of South Dakota School of Law, relates the story a mentor told to him years ago: "A man had gone to live in the desert and pitched his tent in the midst of the Whirling Dervishes. A visiting friend asked him, 'What do you do about the Dervishes?' His response: 'I let them whirl.' "

"I let the difficult people I encounter get what they have off their chests," Mr. Hagemann explains. "When they finish, I ask what they would like me to do for them. If it's reasonable and consistent with . . . policies, I do it; if not, I tell them I can't, and why, and ask them to leave. If they don't, I've been known to walk out of my own office. I have never had that fail to end things."

I've shown you that your difficult people don't have to ruin your life, make you unhappy, or destroy your health. They don't have to be the focus of all your energy. You can control how much they affect you. I've shown you how they affect you, and how to minimize their impact on you. In preparing for this book, one of the people I interviewed was Bill Marriott, president of Marriott International, and asked him how he handles his difficult people. He said, "Everybody's different. Everybody has different things that excite them, drive and push them. You have to orchestrate the differences, play to their strengths, and help them get rid of their weaknesses. If that doesn't work, you have to tell them to share their expertise somewhere else." We've also learned that letting go, or going somewhere else, is an option.

You're a different person now than when you started this book. You've learned about yourself and the difficult people you encounter. You understand more about them

and why they act the way they do. You may not love
them, but at least you can have some compassion for
them, and you'll ultimately learn to accept them.

This journey has just begun. Use the tools you've acquired from this book to know yourself; to throw off the
limitations you've placed on yourself; to forgive yourself
for those times when you felt that you could have handled
things better; and to handle things better in the future.

The *law of successive approximations* says that the more
you do something the better you get. Therefore, starting
off badly isn't bad, as long as you start. Although it might
not be immediately apparent, a simple change in action is
better than no change at all. We know from the Weber-
Fechner law that a little change is a big change, so start
small and aim big.

We've gone into a lot of detail in this book, but it all
comes down to three principles. Use the abbreviation AAS
to remember them:

Acknowledge your difficult people when you can. They
need all the help they can get. When you see them doing
something right, let them know it.

Accept them as much as you can. They are human too,
and struggle with their own self-acceptance. Allow them
the right to exist. The more they see your acceptance of
them, the less they will be difficult. Acceptance automatically takes you out of judgment. The more acceptance you
offer, the higher morale will be, yours *and* theirs.

Set boundaries. Difficult people make a career out of their behaviors. Let them know what is and isn't OK with you. Stand up for yourself without turning into an ape. Let them know how to treat you.

So I turn you loose on the world of aberrant behaviors. I hope that you've had the opportunity to do some experimenting and trials with these techniques and ways of thinking. Remember, people aren't science experiments; what will work with one may not with another. Think of this book not as gospel, but as another search engine in your brain for solutions. When your ideas have run dry, come here for a refill. Pain either sculpts resistance or revelation. Use this book as a reference for revelation. Use the pain and the challenge of your relationships with difficult people as opportunities for learning. If you want more ideas, you can e-mail me at sc@pivpoint.com or visit my website at www.pivpoint.com. No matter what you do, my wish is that you continue to learn, embrace the lessons you are learning, and never again be that lonely fire hydrant in the town full of dogs.

> *You are what your deep, driving desire is.*
> *As your desire is, so is your will.*
> *As your will is, so is your deed.*
> *As your deed is, so is your destiny.*

—The Upanishads, *as translated by Eknath Easwaran*

Bibliography

Anantananda, Swami, *What's on My Mind?* New York: SYDA Foundation, 1996.

Bramson, Robert, *Coping with Difficult People.* New York: Dell, 1988.

Chidvilasananda, Swami, *Inner Treasures.* New York: SYDA Foundation, 1995.

Childre, Doc Lew, *Freeze-Frame.* Boulder Creek, CA: Planetary Publications, 1994.

Cooper, Robert K., and Ayman Sawaf, *Executive EQ: Emotional Intelligence in Leadership and Organizations.* New York: Grosset/Putnam, 1997.

Covey, Stephen R., *The 7 Habits of Highly Effective People.* New York: Simon & Schuster, 1989.

Crum, Thomas F., *The Magic of Conflict.* New York: Touchstone, 1987.

Goleman, Daniel, *Emotional Intelligence.* New York: Bantam, 1995.

Harris, Thomas, M.D., *I'm OK, You're OK: A Practical*

Guide to Transactional Analysis. New York: Harper & Row, 1967.

Jahnke, Roger, *The Healer Within.* San Francisco: HarperCollins, 1997.

Joko Beck, Charlotte, *Everyday Zen.* San Francisco: HarperCollins, 1989.

Kabat-Zinn, Jon, *Wherever You Go, There You Are.* New York: Hyperion, 1994.

Krishnamurti, J., *The Flight of the Eagle.* Madras, India: Krishnamurti Foundation India, 1971.

LeDoux, Joseph, *The Emotional Brain.* New York: Simon & Schuster, 1996.

Muktananda, Swami, *From the Finite to the Infinite.* New York: SYDA Foundation, 1989, 1994.

Paddison, Sara, *The Hidden Power of the Heart.* Boulder Creek, CA: Planetary Publications, 1992.

Peck, Scott, *The Road Less Traveled.* New York: Touchstone, 1978.

Pert, Candace, *Molecules of Emotion: Why You Feel the Way You Feel.* New York: Scribner, 1997.

Schafarman, Steven, *Awareness Heals.* Reading, MA: Addison-Wesley, 1997.

Waitley, Dennis, *Seeds of Greatness.* New York: Simon & Schuster, 1983.

Wilber, Ken, *No Boundary.* Boston: Shambhala, 1979.

Index

Italicized page numbers indicate illustrations

Awareness (*cont.*)
    action, 109
    alert, 21–22
    amygdala responses, 105–6, 111
    body reaction and, 224, 226, 228
    cause and effect relationship, 103–4
    change, 106–10
    emotions, defining, 105–6
    important, feeling, 109–10
    knowledge, getting to, 106–10
    physiological evidence for
        emotions, 105–6, 111
    questions as bridge to, 192–94
    subjective labels (assessment), 107–8
    thought into action, 111
    See also Difficultness, disease of;
        Escape hatches; Expectations,
        changing; Mood, changing;
        Why me?

Backstabbers, 140–42
Beck, Charlotte Joko
    on insanity from our blindness, 4
    on temporary versus permanent
        thinking, 14
Bees, sarcastic, 130–31, 153–54, 254
Behavior and moods relationship, 74–76, 76
Being compliant (BOP method), 83
Belief structure, 248–50
Believing is seeing, 53–54
Blame versus solutions, 41
Body language
    aggressive people, changing for,
        119–20, 121
    language consistency with, 181–82, 194
    See also Body reaction to
        thoughts
Body reaction to thoughts, 221–31
    ABS system for internal stress,
        225–29
    awareness (ABS system for
        internal stress), 224, 226, 228

breathing (ABS system for
    internal stress), 226, 228
IgA, influenced by, 225
listening to, 221–23
perception and context, 224
physiological evidence for
    emotions, 105–6, 111
retraining responses, 224–28
shift (ABS system for internal
    stress), 226–27, 228–29
thought into action, 230–31
Weber-Fechner law, 224
See also Body language; Language
    as tool; Mirror as tool; Power
    of one; Problems and
    solutions
BOP method for mood changing, 83–84, 86
Boundaries, setting, 255–56, 261
Breakdowns, 61–64, 80
Breaking promises, 203
Breathing
    ABS system for internal stress,
        226, 228
    mood changing by, 92–93
Buttons, pushing, 158–59, 161–62

Call or see someone who makes you
    feel good, 86–87
Campbell, Bill, on irritations and
    understanding ourselves, 238
Capability and trust, 246–47
Carefrontation (BOP method), 83–86, 253
Cause and effect relationship of
    awareness, 103–4
Change
    awareness and, 106–10
    inviting versus ordering, 35–37, 36
    yourself and world changes, 25–27, 67–68
Channeling emotional energy, 96–97
Children
    adults versus, on power, 215–16

Photo by Frank Forgione

About the Author

Sandra Crowe, president of Pivotal Point Training and Consulting, is a speaker, author, and seminar leader with over twenty years of experience in the communication field. A certified ontological coach with a masters in applied psychology, she speaks on topics such as dealing with conflict, coaching for results, teams that work, stressless management, and body listening. She consults in Fortune 500 companies such as Marriott, Citicorp, and Sony in addition to government and association-based organizations such as the White House, NASA, and the FBI. She has been written about in the *Washington Post*, the *New York Times*, *Glamour*, *Redbook*, *Good Housekeeping*, and *Men's Health*, and had her own TV show, *Stressbusters*, which aired on a Washington, D.C., station. She has a feature story in the book *Chicken Soup for the Soul at*

Work and writes articles for trade journals and magazines. She has also appeared on the CBS morning news program with Bryant Gumbel, the TV show *To Tell the Truth*, and the local ABC affiliate evening news in Washington, D.C. Her mission is to create awareness of ineffective inter-personal relationships and redirect behavior toward more uplifting interactions. For more information, you can e-mail her at sc@pivpoint.com or visit her website at www.pivpoint.com. Please e-mail her your success stories with difficult people.